VAMPIRES ARE US

VAMPIRES
ARE US

UNDERSTANDING OUR LOVE AFFAIR WITH
THE IMMORTAL DARK SIDE

MARGOT ADLER

WEISER BOOKS
San Francisco, CA / Newburyport, MA

First published in 2014 by Weiser Books
Red Wheel/Weiser, LLC
With offices at:
665 Third Street, Suite 400
San Francisco, CA 94107
www.redwheelweiser.com

ISBN: 978-1-57863-560-3

Library of Congress Cataloging-in-Publication Data available upon request.

Cover design by Jim Warner
Cover photograph shutterstock / locote
Interior by Kathryn Sky-Peck
Typeset in Adobe Garamond

Printed on acid-free paper in the United States of America.
EBM

10 9 8 7 6 5 4 3 2 1

The paper used in this publication meets the minimum requirements of the
American National Standard for Information Sciences—Permanence of Paper for
Printed Library Materials Z39.48-1992 (R1997).

CONTENTS

PREFACE

VAMPIRES! WHY VAMPIRES, you ask? As you will see, once you join me on this strange journey, vampires have always been a metaphor for our fears and concerns, or, as the author Nina Auerbach wrote, "Every age embraces the vampire it needs."

Vampires have been used as a metaphor by everyone from Voltaire to Karl Marx. Bram Stoker's *Dracula,* for example, spoke to the late 19th century's fears of disease and immigration. So what fears and concerns does our current obsession with vampires reveal? What do the popular vampires on television and in novels say about us?

I started this four-year obsession as a meditation on mortality as my husband lay dying of cancer, but I later wandered away from that initial idea onto very different pathways. Besides mortality and immortality, I've been looking at issues of power, sensuality, identity, spirituality, and the environment. And believe it or not, our current crop of vampires has a lot to say about all these issues.

Some of you will pick up this book because you have always been fascinated by vampires; perhaps secretly as a teenager you wanted to be one; perhaps you still do. Others of you will pick up this book because you are curious how a person well-known in both the news media and contemporary Pagan circles, someone with a reasonably intellectual reputation, could be writing on such a frivolous and crazy subject. Hopefully you will be surprised.

Over the last several years I have given a shortened version of these ideas as a sermon in a number of churches. A longer version has been published as an essay, and I have given many talks and presentations. You want the basic idea? The short version goes like this:

Vampires are us. We are as guilt ridden and conflicted over our poisoned relationship to the planet and our continued need for fossil fuels as any of the morally struggling and conflicted vampires we see on television or read about in novels are conflicted over their need for blood.

Most of our current vampires *are* conflicted, and this notion of the struggling-to-be-moral, conflicted vampire really got traction in the late 1960s, at the moment we first saw pictures of the Earth from space and realized our vulnerability and moral complicity.

The first part of this book is the essay that fleshes out these ideas. The second part takes a look at all the books I read during my four-year obsession. They belong to almost every literary genre—from detective fiction to romance, from science fiction to graphic novels, coming–of-age novels, alternate history, and much more. But most people are unaware of this because elite culture disparages genre fiction altogether, so the typical response when I say I've read more than 270 vampire novels is "There *are* 270 vampire novels?" There are actually thousands. So I admit to making an attack on elite literary culture here. I include a summary of almost all the books I came across in four years, and a listing of the best dozen or so, if you want to dip in. I confess that although I do name a number of classics, many novels are more recent, written at the time of our current attraction to vampires.

Lastly, I had a great deal of fun writing this, and reading all these books, even those I wanted to throw across the room! Perhaps I am more accommodating than most, but there were only about 20 out of the 270-plus that I found had absolutely no redeeming value. So, even if you disagree with my thesis, have fun with all this. I did.

PART ONE

Mirror, Mirror

In 1966, Stewart Brand, who went on to publish *The Whole Earth Catalog,* and later founded the Well—arguably the first online community gathering place—the Global Business Network, and other organizations, took an acid trip. You may wonder what Brand's acid trip has to do with vampires and with the question, why do vampires have such traction in our culture now? But just hold on.

Brand gives this account in a 1976 book, *The Sixties.* He was twenty-eight years old and sitting on a rooftop in San Francisco looking out at the horizon. And he remembered something he had heard in a lecture by the architect and futurist Buckminster Fuller, "that people perceived the Earth as flat and infinite, and that was the root of all their misbehavior." Looking at the horizon from the rooftop, and being stoned out of his head, Brand could suddenly see that the Earth was curved. He could think it and feel it.

He suddenly thought that if there was a photograph of the Earth from space, no one would see the planet in the same way. So he printed up several hundred buttons and posters. He thought hard about what phrase to use and finally chose this: "Why haven't we seen a photograph of the whole Earth yet?" It was at the beginning of the Apollo program. He sent the buttons to NASA officials, to members of Congress, to UN and American diplomats, to Soviet scientists, and to people like Marshall McLuhan and Buckminster Fuller.

In fact, there were already a couple of photographs of the whole Earth from space, although not very good ones. They were photographs from satellites, and in black and white. It would take a good color photograph to have real impact. It would take another two years and Apollo 8 before a NASA photographer would give us that picture, now so famous and often called Earthrise. And it would take a few more years until the "blue marble" picture of the Earth was published, becoming perhaps the most reproduced photograph in the world. After he saw the Earthrise picture in 1968, Brand would say that the image showed the Earth as "an island, surrounded by a lot of inhospitable space. And it's so graphic, this little blue, white, green and brown jewel-like icon amongst a quite featureless black vacuum." So, hold that image of the Earth in the back of your mind as we go on a very strange journey. It starts with death.

MORTALITY

TO BE HONEST, I had never been very interested in vampires. I had read Anne Rice's *Interview with the Vampire,* and perhaps *The Vampire Lestat,* and, being a friend of Whitley Strieber, I had read *The Hunger* and loved that most sensual 1983 film with Susan Sarandon, David Bowie, and Catherine Deneuve. But the subject of vampires didn't particularly interest me.

In May of 2009, in a New York airport, right before taking a plane to a conference in Florida, I wanted to pick up a trashy novel, so I bought the first Twilight Saga novel in the airport and I read the second one on the plane ride home. It probably would have ended right there. But ten days after I returned from that conference in May, my world turned upside down. My husband, and life partner of thirty-five years, was diagnosed with terminal stomach cancer. And he was the healthiest man I knew.

It is often said that Anne Rice began her huge saga, the Vampire Chronicles, because she was dealing with the death of her young daughter. I, too, started obsessing on vampire novels because I was thinking about mortality. My husband, who was dying of cancer, was someone who wanted to live forever. He had fought death every moment of his life.

I remember our first date in 1975. It was right out of an old Woody Allen movie. We sat in a Chinese restaurant, and all we talked about was death. Death was not something I had thought about much in my life, but my mother, a smoker for many years, had died horribly of lung cancer in 1970. The cancer went into her brain and her liver. The doctors lied to her and did not tell her she had cancer, which was typical of those times. She was sixty-one and was having the first truly happy relationship of her life, the first fulfilling sexual experience. Her death took place five years before I met my husband, but her illness and death were still open wounds in my life. As an only child of divorce, then in my early twenties, I had to shoulder that burden pretty much alone.

For John, death was the most important fact of his life. Both his parents were killed when two planes collided over Baltimore in the late 1950s. He was sixteen and he had three younger siblings, one of them only four years old. In an instant, his entire life dramatically changed.

He thought about death constantly, and it forever negatively colored his life. He always wondered if death wasn't perhaps the most horrifying and painful event a human being could possibly experience. Perhaps his parents were caught for eternity in that last painful moment of the plane's explosion and fire.

There's a famous Woody Allen line: "I don't want to achieve immortality through my work . . . I want to achieve it through not dying." That's what John wanted. Although to be truthful, he probably wanted both types of immortality. He wanted to live at least two hundred years, and he read everything he could about anti-aging research to help that possibility along.

Death even affected his views on having children. Perhaps having a child was a selfish act, since death was inevitably the result.

As an only child, I had simple fears about children: I was merely afraid I would break the kid somehow, and I also had a deep secret fear that if I had a child, I would become a Stepford wife, a total conformist. I was convinced that it was easy to be a rebellious spirit by oneself, but with the responsibility of kids, and my own need to please others, which was always hidden beneath the surface of my outward strength and confidence, I just *knew* I would cave into society's demands and restrictions.

My husband was an experimental psychologist by training and was making his living as a science journalist who focused on evolution, computers, and quantum physics. And one day John came across the many-worlds hypothesis of quantum physics, and it blew him away. To oversimplify: Every time an atom splits, perhaps there is a parallel world that comes into existence. So perhaps there are parallel worlds where his parents didn't die; perhaps there are several where they are still in the plane; perhaps there are hundreds, maybe even infinite possibilities. And if that's true, then how can you possibly know what death or life is about? So, if you love children and think you would be a good parent, why not go for it? And so we did.

John and I had each read about a thousand science fiction novels before we met. We both believed that science fiction opened vistas; it allowed so many different ways to imagine life, work, and love. At the time we met, we each believed we would travel to the stars together. That seems such a crazy idea today, but it didn't seem bizarre in the 1970s as we watched spaceships land on the moon. When we saw the film *2001: A Space Odyssey,* we looked at the moon base depicted in the film and thought, *Oh, how awful, how corporate, but we will do it better.* John worried so much about the abuse of science and the militarization of space that he never created a career that might have taken him toward the space effort. But he looked at the stars with his five telescopes and we talked about all the wild things that might be possible: colonies in space and cryogenically preserving our bodies. A lot of the ideas were way out there, but there was never a boring moment in thirty-five years.

John definitely had the "high tech" view of death. As I said, he read every article on aging research he could get his hands on, and he took more than a dozen vitamins, anti-oxidants, and supplements. He was a runner who was in perfect health. He never smoked, was fit, and, unlike me, never did any drugs in his youth. He ate salads, yogurt, wheat germ, and fruit, and some occasional meat, mostly chicken. He drank a glass of red wine for resveratrol. And he was cautious. His best friend died in a rafting accident in Chile; John would never take such risks. He thought he would live a long time, given scientific and medical advances. His attitude was definitely "rage, rage against the dying of the light."

And then he got the kind of stomach cancer that usually attacks people in Asian countries who eat spicy foods. He had only two weeks of symptoms before he was diagnosed, and after nine months of chemotherapy and radiation, he died. In the end I think he felt cheated and betrayed by all those supplements he took.

There was a definite tension between John and me over our views on death, a tension I didn't really understand until after he died. I, at the same moment he was fighting death, had more of an Earth-centered Pagan perspective that went something like this: We are all part of the life cycle. Like a seed, we are born, we sprout, we grow, we mature, and later we decay, making room for future generations, who, like seedlings, are reborn through us. This is all part of nature's dance. To everything there is a season, as the old psalm goes, and that should be enough.

As for the persistence of consciousness, deep down I thought, *How can we know?* Perhaps we simply return to the elements. We become earth, air, fire, and water. In fact, I remember reading a book on the *I Ching* by the feminist author Barbara Walker in which she argued that the ancient meaning of the four elements was that each was a way the ancients went to their death: we were left for carrion in the air, we were buried in the earth, we were burnt on the pyre, and we were buried at sea. That seemed just about right.

So there was a continuing, mostly unexpressed tension between my own Pagan world view that accepted death as natural and the high tech, futurist views of my late husband who fought death with every breath. But neither of us was totally wedded to a single vision. And way down deep there was a part of me that also wanted to live forever.

We talked about the possibilities of life extension. We wondered about genetic manipulation. At the same time, I traveled through the world of earth-based spirituality with people who honored the crone and talked about death as a natural part of life.

What I now realize is that the tensions about death that existed between my husband, John, and me, are the very same tensions that exist in some of the most interesting vampire novels. Vampires of myth and literature embody a complicated split. They have near immortality and yet are tragically frozen in time. They cannot grow and change like the seasons or, in most descriptions, birth new life, and yet they have increased strength, agility, heightened senses, and often the wisdom that can come with extreme age, although it's often mixed with a cynical, jaundiced view of life. Rosalie, who desperately wants a child and bemoans her frozen state in the Twilight Saga, is asking the same questions posed in books like *Tuck Everlasting* or Olaf Stapledon's famous science fiction novel *Last and First Men*. Stapledon published this novel in 1930, and it describes the far-flung future of humanity over two billion years and almost twenty different human species. But several of them play with the issue of longevity. One species lives for nearly two hundred years, and far into the future, a fifth species of humankind lives for thousands of years and essentially achieves immortality. No species, however, avoids tragedy or the sorrows that are part of almost all human lives.

This tension over death is part of who we are. Human beings want to be part of nature, but at the same time we have a deep and passionate urge to persist, to live forever, to cheat death, to push the edge of the envelope, to be more. *Further,* as the old hippie slogan went.

Vampires let us play with death and mortality. They let us ponder what it would mean to live a truly long life. How would that change one's view of everything in society? Playing with the idea of a long life allows us to ask questions we usually bury, except in science fiction. What does one value more and what does one value less with a long human life? Would we become bored? Would we become more or less compassionate? Does the vampire's long life allow a different vision of the world? Would having a long life allow us to see the world differently, imagine social structures differently, and have a longer view? Would it increase or decrease reverence for the planet? Is the vampire's frozen "life" sterile, as Rosalie opines in *Twilight*? Does life mean something only when it is part of a larger cycle of birth, growth, decay, death, and the birth of new life? Is there a beauty that comes only from the cycles of which we are a part? Or is the heroic struggle imagined by every superhero a worthy one—a symbol of our striving to break through our human and planetary limitations?

When we look at mortality and immortality through the eyes of teens and young adults, there is something else going on. Our culture does not do death well. Western culture still has few good rites of passage for death compared to indigenous cultures, with the possible exception of a good Irish wake. I am reminded of a 1990 young adult vampire novel called *The Silver Kiss* by Annette Curtis Klause. The vampire aspect is almost an afterthought in this book, although the vampire is a typical lonely outsider, beautiful and ethereal. The protagonist, Zoe, is an only child whose mother is in and out of the hospital with cancer. As a result, her father has become increasingly remote. Wanting to "protect" their daughter, the parents allow Zoe at the hospital for only brief moments, and no one speaks about death: the elephant in the living room. When Zoe meets Simon, a three-hundred-year-old vampire, there is, to be sure, one ecstatic kiss, but what really takes place is a bonding between two lonely individuals who can talk about pain, loss, and the death of loved ones. At the end of the book, Zoe has her first real talk with each of her parents about the reality of death.

The vampire leaves by the end of the novel; her mother dies; Zoe moves to San Francisco and goes on with her life. The mother is not saved by turning her into a vampire; there is no passionate sexual union; Zoe and Simon don't end up in each other's lives except in their dreams. But the story is clearly a vehicle to discuss topics so often denied. And the vampire, the symbol of the outsider, becomes a way for Zoe to finally come inside.

Many of us saw countless Disney films as children. Think of how often the mother dies in those films (*Bambi, The Fox and the Hound, Finding Nemo*), or the father (*The Lion King*), or both parents (*Tarzan*). Given how often we encountered death in fairy tales and films as children, why do so many parents clam up about death during the teenage years and during adolescence, which is often the time when death becomes real for their children? Are the huge number of paranormal and vampire young adult novels, in small part, a way for teens to have those discussions about death and the meaning of existence that are not taking place at home?

So my own vampire journey started with the issue of mortality. And a year and a half after I began that journey, at the end of 2010, I began my own battle with cancer, which continues, although so far I feel in good health. But I realized very quickly that death and even the wish for immortality did not explain the millions of readers, movie viewers, and television watchers who were devouring vampire stories. Or the billions of dollars that Hollywood and the television industry were spending each year to serve these stories up for a willing and paying audience. I also realized my own fascination, even love of vampires, was about more than a desire to live forever. Truth be told, I wanted to *be* one. And I was not alone.

Of course, everyone said to me, "Isn't the whole vampire obsession really about sex?" And if you read some of the more popular vampire romances, you might come away with that idea. But as I began to read about the vampire fantasies of others, I realized that while romance and sensuality were abundant, sex, as most people think about it, as intercourse, was not nearly as prevalent as you might think.

There *are* dreadful vampire romances with repetitive and formulaic sex scenes, and really bad writing, with phrases like "he filled me" over and over until you want to barf. And the heroines in these books are gorgeous, flawless beings, women with thin waists and large bosoms. The men are dark and mysterious, and always, always, there are perfect orgasms every time, aided by telepathic communication. We should be so lucky! But most of the vampire fantasies experienced by women and men are very different.

In Martin V. Riccardo's fascinating book *Liquid Dreams of Vampires* (1997), he spent six years collecting the dreams and fantasies of men and women who found themselves obsessed by and attracted to vampires. Most of the men and women said they not only were attracted to vampires, they wanted to *be* one, or they fantasized that they *were* vampires. Some of them wished for immortality; some expressed a fear of death and aging. Many identified with the vampire as rebel and alien, the lonely outsider. Some expressed a love of the vampire's strength, their lack of ties to the world, their lack of commitment—the sense of power and lack of limitations. Sex was definitely secondary.

Katherine Ramsland, the biographer of Anne Rice, writes in *Piercing the Darkness: Undercover with Vampires in America Today*

(1998) that when she was young she was fascinated by *Dracula*. "I wanted to feel what he felt when he went after his prey. I went to bed each night with my arms crossed over my chest in the hope that I would waken as a vampire. I told people I was 403 years old. Without knowing how to articulate it, I sensed there was some visceral quality in the vampire's experience that would enhance life and make me feel as if I were part of something much larger than myself."

Some people in Riccardo's book do talk about love and sensuality, but very few of the fantasies mention sexual intercourse or penetration. The eroticism more often involves biting and sharing blood. And while there are plenty of people who will give you a Freudian analysis of this, how these people are "fixated in the oral stage," anyone who has cut their finger as a child and licked it knows there is a certain comfort in connecting with that juice of life.

In many novels, vampires can't have normal sexual intercourse. In Stoker's time you would not have put a sex scene in a novel, but if you think of the vampire novels by Anne Rice and Chelsea Quinn Yarbro, written in the 1970s and 1980s, a time when explicit sex was common in literature, there is no intercourse. Unlike many of the current vampire romance novels, the novels by Rice and Yarbro emphasize—like the fantasies Riccardo obtained in his interviews—a sharing of blood, and a feeling of total ecstatic union, which Riccardo says, "implies feelings of connection, intimacy, sensuality, and arousal without any direct connection to sexual intercourse." In other words, he says, the vampire is a sensual rather than a purely sexual creature.

In 1976, I had a totally ecstatic experience for three days. Shere Hite had just come out with her book *The Hite Report*. It was not an academic study and critics called it unscientific. But women like me loved it. What she did was interview hundreds, perhaps more than a thousand women, whom she did not identify. Hite claimed that some 70 percent of the women she surveyed did not achieve orgasm through penetration, although most experienced orgasm easily through masturbation, and desperately wanted more foreplay in their relationships. When I read that book at the age of thirty, I was high for three days; I felt "normal" for only the second time since my teenage years. The first time, several years earlier, was during intimate discussions with a group of women in a consciousness-raising group—an experience shared by thousands of women in the feminist movement. For many of us it was more deeply life-changing than any therapy.

You could argue that the vampire is clearly speaking up for a more female-centered form of lovemaking and sensuality. But it's not sex as we tend to think of it in popular culture. Riccardo even argues—although this goes way too far—that when we see novels where women are taken by force by vampires, it is done with such elegance and style, they don't think of it as rape.

But I am going to argue that just as rape is only superficially about sex, and really about power, so, underneath much of the romance and sexuality that we see in vampire fiction and films is a deeper exploration of power and its abuses. And power is something that we all tussle with. And it's something most of us want more of.

POWER

"There is no good or bad, there is just power."

BUFFY SUMMERS

NOW, HERE'S THE TRUTH. During the time I was obsessing over vampire novels, I was also playing with my own vampire fantasy. Every time I tried to write it down, I realized how bad it was from a literary point of view—it was a very mediocre example of *Twilight* fan fiction. I took the character of Alice Cullen, Edward's psychic sister, and morphed her into a different place and time, seeking family, friends, and graduate school in a world where vampires had—like in *True Blood*—come "out of the coffin" into the real world. My Alice was less psychic, but she had the powers of vampires in *Twilight*: speed, agility, strength, acute senses, the wisdom of age with the looks of youth, and an almost eternal life. Deep down, they were powers I wanted.

"If you had power over others, how would you use it? That," says Amy Smith, an English professor at the University of the Pacific in California, "is the central question in almost every good vampire novel and film."

Smith teaches a course on vampires in film. And she has thought a lot about power. She's a Quaker who also teaches a course on the literature of war. Smith says almost every good vampire film is about the use and abuse of power. Here's her argument: the central question in so many of these films and novels is, now that you are a vampire and have extraordinary powers do you say, "We are at the top of the food chain; we can do what we want. Humans are food," or do you say, "We were once human, how can we treat humans as cattle"? Smith says the struggle at the heart of almost every vampire movie is the old struggle: does might make right? And it is the same tension we have in our normal lives: does having more money than others, or more power or status, give us the right to use it to dominate others?

Most of us are in conflict over issues of power. We want it; we distrust it; we get twisted by it; we abuse it; we struggle with our love and hate of it. And in a shifting, changing world, we often feel powerless.

It's easy to see why teenagers, who often feel vulnerable, powerless, and invisible in the world, are attracted to vampires. They experience the abuse of power more clearly than grown-ups who have acclimated to cultural norms and keep telling them, "That's just how the world works, honey." Bullied by other children, or becoming bullies themselves, under the thumb of parents and school, young people are in the best time of their lives to understand the abuses of power in society—and to imagine another world where these issues are resolved differently.

When J. Gordon Melton, author of *The Vampire Book: The Encyclopedia of the Undead,* the most comprehensive encyclopedia on the subject, talks about his lifelong fascination with vampires, he says that growing up in an evangelical community, he understood, innately, that there was a difference between "evil" and "dark." He was fascinated with what Jungians would call "the shadow," the often hidden unconscious parts of the self that we often deny, parts of us that are sometimes negative but often deeply creative. Also, as a teenage boy, he felt powerless, and vampires were powerful; he was sexually unsure, and vampires had sexual magnetism. Vampires were everything he wasn't.

Anne Rice, the author of the Vampire Chronicles, and one of the first authors to really flesh out the morally conflicted vampire, has the best description I have ever read of why vampires have such power and traction for teens today. Of course, she says, vampires reflect the troubles in our society, our dreams, our fears, but "right now," she wrote to me in an email, "the vampire reflects more than anything else the tremendous need of adolescents and young people to embrace their monstrous and outsider status in our society, their refusal to see themselves as the criminal class they are often forced into being where their established rites of passage are understood to be forbidden sex, illegal drugs, and sometimes criminal rebellion."

The vampire, she concludes, "the metaphor for the outsider in all of us, is romanticized by them because [my italics] *they so desperately need to find a noble path through the hideous passage that Western culture has set up for them.*"

Meditate on that line for a moment. Let's face it, for many teenagers, high school is a time when they feel most powerless. High school is often a horror, made worse by the pressures of cliques; consumer culture; issues of money, status, clothes, class, race, popularity, sports. Not to mention the academic pressure placed on teens by parents and school authorities. Sure, many sail through this period seemingly unscathed. But for others, vampires are a perfect antidote to the pull and pressures of parental and corporate culture.

For me, high school was bleak, a blur; I don't even remember the names of most of my classmates. And I went to one of the most famous public high schools in the nation—the High School of Music and Art, which later joined with Performing Arts to become LaGuardia, and is known by many because of the movie *Fame*. Although we had a fabulous assortment of interesting students and didn't have to contend with jock culture, when our senior prom was canceled for very odd reasons, I breathed a long sigh of relief. I had no one to go with.

Think about the Cullen family in *Twilight* for a moment, having to do high school over and over. Think about having to go to your senior prom five times in five different schools. Now that's a real horror story! And it's all about navigating *the hideous passage that Western Culture has set up for them.*

And part of navigating that passage is coming to terms with issues of money, status, class, the lure of celebrity, and so many myths in our culture. The lust for power and status draws one in like an addictive drug, promising false happiness, perhaps like the glamour from the eyes of a mythic vampire. This may give us a clue to why the image of the vampire is so often used to depict robber barons and corporate raiders on Wall Street. Using the word "vampire" in that political way goes back to the 17th century.

POWER and POLITICS

I REPORTED ON Occupy Wall Street for NPR during 2011–12. I was a political activist in my youth; I was arrested in the Free Speech Movement at Berkeley in 1964; I worked for civil rights and black voter registration in Mississippi in 1965; I was in the streets of Chicago in 1968. When I began to report on Occupy Wall Street, I was fascinated by how creative OWS protesters were during many of their demonstrations—more creative than what I remember of demonstrations in the 1960s. My favorite scene during a protest march was a group of nine men dressed in Brooklyn Dodger baseball uniforms with the word "Tax" substituted for the word "Brooklyn." They were accompanied by a dancer with a huge Hula-Hoop with the word "loopholes" written on it and a banker with a top hat carrying money bags. But I also noticed that in several parades and demonstrations, OWS demonstrators wore costumes depicting themselves as vampire bankers—complete with fangs, white makeup, and black capes, an image of corporate America sucking the lifeblood out of society.

Since the economic meltdown in 2008, journalists writing about Wall Street have often used phrases that compare transparency and regulation with the light of the sun that would kill a mythic vampire. Writers would describe Wall Street executives as fleeing before the shining light of public scrutiny. Here is Rachel

Lewis of the group Public Citizen writing a blog in *The Huffington Post* in the fall of 2011:

> It's dark enough outside as it is. The economy is weak, most wallets are thin. What Sanders released was just one day's worth of trading data, and it's three years old at that but—like a single ray of sunlight—it's already enough to make the vampires scream. Time to summon the sun. They may have fangs but we have the numbers. Who else is ready to take on the vampires of Wall Street?

There are many such examples. An issue of *Veterans Today* has a cartoon of someone putting a stake in the heart of a Wall Street trader. The accompanying article, by Allen L. Roland, says, "unregulated financial vampires are sucking the blood out of Wall Street and leaving America vulnerable to another immense financial collapse." The article goes on to say that the resurrection of the Glass-Steagall Act would be the appropriate stake in the heart.

There's a reference to vampires as political and economic bloodsuckers all the way back in 1688, in an essay by Charles Forman, "Some Queries and Observations upon the Revolution of 1688 and Its Consequences." Finally published in 1741, Forman writes about "the Vampires of the Publick, and the Riflers of the Kingdom."

The French writer and philosopher Voltaire has a listing for vampires in his 1764 *Philosophical Dictionary*. After saying they are clearly not real, he adds, "We never heard a word of vampires in London, nor even at Paris. I confess that in both these cities there were stock-jobbers, brokers, and men of business, who sucked the blood of the people in broad daylight; but they were not dead, though corrupted. These true suckers lived not in cemeteries, but in very agreeable palaces."

Friedrich Engels, who often collaborated with Karl Marx, talked about the "vampire property-holding class" in *The Condition of the Working Class in England,* first published in 1845. Karl Marx continued the notion of capitalist bloodsuckers in his essay "The Eighteenth Brumaire of Louis Napoleon," first published in 1852 (Part 7). Marx wrote that "The bourgeois social order . . . has become a vampire that sucks out its heart-blood and its very brain, and throws it into the alchemist's pot of capital." He also describes capitalism as "vampire-like" in his huge work *Capital.*

Vampires are also associated with power politics and political gamesmanship in today's modern vampire novels, unlike other supernatural beings in fiction—such as werewolves, witches*, or zombies. One of the reasons vampires find political intrigue almost as thirst quenching as blood is their long life. Let's face it, political strategy becomes vastly more interesting if you have hundreds of years to move your chess pieces.

Carrie Vaughn has written a whole series of books about Kitty Norville, a woman who outs herself as a werewolf on her weekly live midnight radio show. Kitty takes calls and gives advice to all kinds of people, with an emphasis on the supernatural. She solves crimes and has complex relationships with werewolves and vampires, and one vampire becomes a close ally. But all the really important political intrigue is vampire-inspired. In *Kitty and the Silver Bullet*, Kitty ends up as a pawn in a game run by a powerful vampire actress who is the first vampire to publicly reveal herself on Kitty's radio

---

* The words "Pagan" and "Witch" should always be capitalized when they are used as religious terms, just like "Catholic" or "Jew." In the works described in this book, however, the word "witch" is not always describing a religious identity. It does for some characters, but not for others. For the sake of consistency, the word will not be capitalized here.

show, but her true goal is more sinister. We learn a new phrase: "the Long Game." Vampires live so long, their intrigues can last over centuries. In *Kitty Raises Hell,* she becomes the target of a two-thousand-year-old vampire from Roman times who seems to be a key to the Long Game. And in subsequent novels there are hints of a Long Game war.

Jeff Gillenkirk's wonderful political novel, *Pursuit of Darkness,* imagines an election somewhat similar to 2012, and it involves a powerful GOP political operative, Jonathan Drees, who is clearly a kind of Karl Rove figure. Drees claims to be a two-hundred-year-old vampire. Our protagonist—an alcoholic *Washington Post* reporter—has no way to prove this, but he comes to believe that there are vampires in the halls of power and in the FBI, and that they have their own long-term agenda, part of which is simply assuring that the world continues to have a plentiful blood supply. This same idea figures in the recent book and movie *Abraham Lincoln: Vampire Hunter.* Here, vampires are seen supporting slavery during the Civil War for similar reasons.

The Chicagoland Vampires series, by Chloe Neill, is filled with—you guessed it—Chicago politics. Our heroine, Merit, comes from a powerful Chicago political family; she is turned into a vampire against her will and, it turns out, for political reasons by a member of her own family. The vampires are organized into houses, almost like fraternities, but with more power. There are political skirmishes between houses and between other supernatural beings, and Chicago's mayor and other politicians are involved.

And of course, let's not forget E. L. James's ruthless CEO, Christian Grey, in the best-seller *Fifty Shades of Grey.* That book started out as a piece of *Twilight* fan fiction, a reminder that vampires and the politics of Wall Street are closer than most imagine.

Vampires have long been a symbol of abusive economic power, and broader issues of power and identity are at the heart of many of the most popular vampire films and television shows of the last twenty years. Occasionally, they even re-imagine power. Take *Buffy the Vampire Slayer,* for example.

I confess I never watched *Buffy* originally. I even scoffed at it. But when I began to be obsessed with vampires, I watched all seven seasons and loved it. Here is something most people don't know: more than half the scholarly articles on vampires are about *Buffy*. The magazine *Slayage* still publishes scholarly articles about *Buffy*, more than six years after the show ceased production.

Many feminist scholars have noted that *Buffy the Vampire Slayer* has a totally different notion of power, what feminists have always called "power from within" as opposed to "power over." Buffy starts as a simple high school student, pretty much a Valley Girl, who is unexpectedly called to fight evil as the Chosen One. But by the seventh and last season of the television show, everything is in question: Buffy's leadership, her authority, her morals, her power. The women who join her to be vampire slayers reject her power when it is based on hierarchy. It's a lesson that Buffy, herself, learns late. "It's a hard truth but there has to be a single voice," she says at one point. But, as the seventh and last season winds down, Buffy is forced to listen, to communicate, and to change "from an I to a we," as Elizabeth Rambo in an article in *Slayage* puts it, until Buffy comes to reject authoritarian power, even her own. By the end of the show, she shares power with all potential vampire slayers and becomes a symbol of feminist, non-patriarchal leadership.

Joss Whedon, the creator of Buffy, describes what happens to Buffy as a shift toward communal power—a shift away from Buffy as a central character to "Okay, it's great that you've worshipped this one iconic character, but find it in yourself, everybody." Whedon has always said he is a feminist. He has said that the mission of the show was to show the joy of female power, having it, using it, sharing it. At the end of season seven, Buffy says, "In every generation one slayer is born because a bunch of men who died thousands of years ago made up that rule. They were power-ful men. . . . So I say we change the rule. I say my power should be our power." In one interview, Whedon said he always felt bad for the blond girl in the horror movie who keeps getting killed. "She was always more interesting to me than the other women. She was fun; she had sex; she was vivacious. But then she would get punished for it." So he thought, "What if the girl goes into the dark alley. And the monster follows her. And she destroys him." You can argue that the story of Buffy is really the story of how a woman learns to become a leader in the best sense.

Of course, Buffy has always had supernatural power, but not economic power; in several shows she has an absolutely demean-ing fast food job. Before that she is an abominable student, often in trouble in a school so deadening and dehumanizing that it is no coincidence that the portal to the world of demons, the Hell-mouth, is underneath the school.

It may not surprise some people that *Buffy the Vampire Slayer* looks at issues of power; but I would argue that even the Twilight Saga is more about power and identity than sex or sexual abstinence.

Who is Bella in *Twilight*? She is an only child of divorce, living in a town with not much going on. Her father is a cop. She's middle-middle class; the dad's a nice-enough guy, but there isn't much happening in the way of deep reflection or conversation. Bella's mom is living in Florida, married to a minor league ballplayer, and there's not much going on there either. Whether she lives in Florida or comes back to Forks, Washington, life is fairly barren. School isn't very interesting, and she's pretty much alone— again the outsider. She's klutzy and dresses down. The two families that come into her life and change her world bring excitement and attractive men for sure but also intellectual stimulation and very different notions of power, identity, and class.

Jacob's world is a large extended family filled with indigenous people and tribal lore, not to mention ancient ritual. It's a working-class family; it's a huge clan, one with long traditions, wise leaders, and superhuman powers. Edward's family is also a large, extended one, although one based on those who have been rescued by Dr. Cullen; it's a family of choice. It is upper class, super-educated, rich, and worldly. They speak many languages, play classical music on the piano, and display multiple degrees on the wall. And, of course, there are all those otherworldly powers and abilities and even near immortality. Both families are more interesting choices than Bella's family of birth. And both families have a secret, outsider life. If there is a Mormon dimension to Stephenie Meyer's work, it may not be as much about repressed sex and teen abstinence—as many feminists have argued—as much as the longing for and belief in large extended families, not to mention, as we will see later, a certain kind of spirituality. As for Bella, she, like so many teens, feels like an alien who is more at home in an inhuman world than a human one. She wears sweatshirts and drives an old truck. And as she negotiates the school lunchroom, and the upcoming prom, Bella is a perfect case of someone who, in Anne Rice's words, is seeking a "noble path through the hideous passage that Western culture has set up for them."

The PERSECUTED OTHER

WHEN I WAS A CHILD I spent hours daydreaming. Almost any historical or science fiction novel could transport me to another time and place. I probably spent at least two hours a day in strange, confabulated worlds—no, let's be honest, perhaps four, even six. I often returned to the current fantasy of the week or month while riding the subway to school. In fact, I often had no idea how I ended up at the entrance to my high school, which involved climbing some ten or twelve flights of steps through a park in Harlem. I was totally in another world, oblivious.

I was an only child, with a number of good friends, but not particularly popular. I was certainly not part of any "in" clique. Social events spelled anxiety; the fantasy worlds I created and controlled were, like food, much more comforting.

Although I was enchanted by the worlds depicted by Tolkien, and the romances of King Arthur's court, there was really only one basic fantasy for me, something I have come to call the "Persecuted Other."

As a child of the political left, during the Cold War, in the 1950s and early 1960s, a "pink diaper baby" at the very least, one of those Persecuted Other fantasies involved being the daughter of the Soviet foreign minister Andrei Gromyko. I am not kidding! And even telling you this makes me cringe!

In the fantasy, I was looked upon as strange and different, speaking a different language, trying to win friends despite the distrust of everyone around me. I drew pictures in my diary of Yvonne Gromyko, a character I created. Now, this was during the height of the Cold War and anti-communist hysteria. My family's views were definitely socialist. Although no one in my family was a member of the Communist Party—in fact, my mother had been told she was too much of an anarchist to be allowed to join—we were definitely "Reds." When John F. Kennedy was assassinated, instead of weeping, my family quaked in terror, since, like Lee Harvey Oswald, JFK's presumed and accused killer, my mother was a member of an organization called Fair Play for Cuba. So, as I listened to my high school social studies teacher's patriotic and anti-communist views and looked at the headlines in the newspapers, it was easy to believe I was an alien in a hostile world. Those feelings were clearly part of the inspiration for the Gromyko fantasy.

Another fantasy was having special powers that made me odd and unusual: telepathic abilities, for example, which I may have taken from a John Brunner science fiction novel, or the ability to fly. Science fiction novels are filled with stories of people who are persecuted for their abilities or ideas, or who are strangers in a strange land. One of my favorite novels is *The Dispossessed* by Ursula K. Le Guin, in which the protagonist comes down to a somewhat fascistic Earth from a gentler, egalitarian, and more anarchist society and tries to comprehend the world around him.

By the time I entered college in the tumultuous year 1964, much of my fantasizing had abated, although it would rise again more than forty years later as vampire fantasies during my husband's illness and death.

But as I watched the power, popularity, and general attraction of superheroes in both comics and films who are persecuted, like the X-Men or Harry Potter, and as I watched the fervor for *The Hunger Games* as well as recent remakes of *Spider-Man* and *Batman,* I realized that my own fantasies were not so different from the feelings of so many young people: the sense of being different, an outsider. Like them, I was exactly that "other," seeking friendship but also thinking I had deep secrets that had to be hidden. For many young people, thinking you have such dark secrets, whether true or not, is really about a feeling that you are different down to your core and that your own inner life marks you as being something other than what the expectations of society and family might dictate.

Go to a site like Amazon, and read the citizen reviews of Colin Wilson's *The Outsider.* Although written back in 1956 when Wilson was only twenty-four, you will find current reviews by young people who say over and over, "This is the book that changed my life." The Outsider, Wilson writes, feels more deeply, has awakened to chaos, has a sense of strangeness. Most people keep up a pretense "to themselves, to others; their respectability, their philosophy, their religion, are all attempts to gloss over, to make look civilized and rational something that is savage, unorganized, irrational. He is an Outsider," Wilson writes, "because he stands for Truth."

If you look at Young Adult fiction, so many of the themes are about fighting persecution, gaining confidence, and winning a place of security and happiness, despite being complex and different. Whether it's *The Hunger Games* or *Twilight,* gaining one's sense of power and identity is paramount.

Vampires, like other superheroes we read about or see in films, are often both powerful and persecuted. Vampires are one current incarnation of the Persecuted Other. They are outsiders and dark rebels with enormous strengths. They are strong and agile, have heightened senses and the ability to heal fast, and they defeat death with a near immortality. They also have the kind of power to take on the world that we can only fantasize about. If we feel disempowered, vampires represent power. Yet they are not accepted by the culture; they are persecuted monsters. That's one of the clear attractions of television series like *Buffy, True Blood, The Vampire Diaries, Forever Knight,* and *Being Human.*

I have now read more than 270 vampire novels over the last three and a half years. And when my husband became ill with cancer and I sat by his bedside while he slept, I not only read, but also began fantasizing again, almost as powerfully as I had in my youth.

I don't think I would ever have dared to talk publicly about these daydreams when I was in my teens or twenties. How embarrassed I was in those teen years; how I would cringe when I thought about what people were thinking about me, how they would judge the way I looked or dressed. And of course, those hundreds of thousands riding on the subway with me could have cared less; their thoughts were their own. They had no interest in whether my armpits smelled or my hair was combed. Now, in my late sixties, I still cringe a bit, when writing about these fantasies, but age, and the confidence that comes with it, means I don't have to care so much about what people think about my guilty pleasures, obsessions, and the totally crazy and stupid things I have done over the years. Example: I once walked into a hair salon with a picture of Alice Cullen from the first *Twilight* movie and said, "I would like something pixie-ish like that." "You would need a lot of hair spray to achieve that effect," was the reply. We laughed.

As I said, the vampire fantasy that took hold of me after I read *Twilight* and all the Charlaine Harris novels (the Southern Vampire Mysteries series, now immortalized on television as *True Blood*) was clearly in the Persecuted Other tradition—a total reimagining of the Cullen family in the Twilight Saga. I easily changed names, locations, and professions but kept the idea in *Twilight* of a scientist vampire who creates a family of choice through rescue. The characters change and grow as vampires "come out" into the world, just as they do in the *True Blood* world, except, unlike Louisiana's Bon Temps, it's more my world: an intellectual, academic, and coastal world. In my version, as the legal situation for vampires changes, and they "come out," they are desperate to discover their true life work, which, of course, includes social activism and actual professions, with driver's licenses and passports to prove their real age.

Many adventures arise from all this, but, as I said, every time I have tried to write them down, I have hated the results. Perhaps, after so many years of journalism and some crazy belief on my part about the power of facts, fiction does not come easily to me.

But here's the thing. All these things I have told you still didn't answer my most basic question: why do vampires have such traction in our culture now? I was still perplexed. As I thought about all these issues—power and identity and the outsider as persecuted rebel, the fear of mortality and the desire to defeat death—none of them gave me the answer I was looking for; none of them really explained why vampires are so popular right now. So one day, I simply took all the most popular vampires on television and film and wrote their names in a line on a piece of paper: Bill Compton and Eric Northman of *True Blood,* Stefan and Damon of *The Vampire Diaries,* Angel and Spike in *Buffy the Vampire Slayer,* Mitchell and Aidan in the English and American versions of *Being Human,* Mick St. John in *Moonlight,* Henry Fitzroy in Tanya Huff's Blood books series, Nicholas Knight in *Forever Knight,* and of course the Cullen family in *Twilight.* And a light bulb went off.

The STRUGGLE to BE MORAL

I WAS VERY STRUCK by a line in Nina Auerbach's book *Our Vampires, Ourselves.* She wrote, "Every age embraces the vampire it needs." So I started thinking about what we truly need right now. I thought about my own journey into Paganism, Wicca, and earth-based spirituality. I had started that journey because I loved nature, and as a person in my twenties, I was totally fired up by the ecology movement and by fears that we were endangering the planet. I was looking for a religion of nature that would have few dogmas and would be free thinking and free spirited. It was right after the first Earth Day in 1970. The needs I saw were for planetary survival and the health of the forests, the air, and the water. I became totally convinced we were in a pretty desperate situation. The fate of the planet was my fear and concern at the time.

Getting back to Auerbach's idea, I began to see that vampires have always reflected the fears and concerns of an age. Take Bram Stoker's *Dracula,* for example. "It was written at the end of the 19th century, at a time when England had some of the largest ports in the world," says the historian Benita Blessing, who teaches modern European history at the University of Vienna, in Austria. "Here you have a ship arriving from Eastern Europe, bearing soil from another country, and a plague-like person who is going to bring death and destruction. The concerns at that time were foreign illnesses and unwanted immigrants. What *Dracula* is about," she says, "is the fear of what we might today call globalization." Dracula was the perfect image to reflect those fears, an Eastern European monster, dark, mysterious, and alien.

You can do this for many periods of history. The first vampire short story in the English language, "The Vampyre" by John William Polidori, was published in 1819, but it was begun three years before, on the same weekend, in the same château in Switzerland where Mary Shelley began her work on *Frankenstein*. It was a time when the scientific revolution was bringing up fears of science replacing God. To give one more example, in the 1980s, just as the AIDS epidemic was spreading, there were a slew of vampire novels that saw vampirism as an infection, a disease. "It's almost this perfect vessel," says Eric Nuzum, the author of a very fun survey, *The Dead Travel Fast: Stalking Vampires from Nosferatu to Count Chocula*. "If you want to understand any moment in time, or any cultural moment, just look at their vampires."

None of this is totally surprising, but why are vampires attractive to us *now*? What are the fears and concerns they speak to? What kind of vampires are we creating now, and why? How are they different from those that went before?

So I looked again at my list of popular vampires over the last twenty years. Angel and Spike, the Cullen family, Eric and Bill, Stefan and Damon, Mitchell and Aidan, Mick St. John, Nicholas Knight, Henry Fitzroy. And the light bulb that went off was this: they are all guilt ridden and conflicted. Unlike many of the vampires of old, they are struggling desperately to be moral, despite their history as predators and their need for blood. Sometimes they succeed; more often they fail. But they are always conflicted.

There has been a long tradition in vampire literature of the "good guy vamp." It can be seen in the figure of the Comte de Saint-Germain in the novels by Chelsea Quinn Yarbro and in Fred Saberhagen's portrait of Dracula as a positive hero, first in *The Dracula Tape* and then in many subsequent novels. But what we now see in hundreds of books, movies, comics, and television shows that feature vampires is the conflicted vampire, what I have been calling the desperately-struggling-to-be-moral-despite-being-predators vampire: the one that represents our own current moral struggle.

Vampires are exactly us right now, as we continue to wage wars, consume energy, and find ourselves unable and unwilling to figure out solutions to global planetary issues. To be blunt, we are sucking the lifeblood out of the planet. Some of us think we can get around all this by lowering our carbon footprint, riding bicycles, and recycling, but the truth is that the solutions to our large problems are mostly systemic, and frankly, none of these individual actions do much to change the world. We live compromised lives. Whitley Strieber, author of *The Hunger*, goes further. "Our prey is the planet," he told me. If so, vampires are us, and the issue before us is how we can learn to use our formidable powers without destroying the planet for future generations.

You could argue that we are as addicted to oil and fossil fuels as any vampire is addicted to blood. Eight U.S. presidents in a row have earnestly said they would end our country's dependence on oil, or certainly foreign oil, and most of them have meant it, in the same way smokers believe they will quit. And while we are lessening our dependence on foreign oil, fossil fuels still dominate our economy and infrastructure. The way we live, travel, and work continues to compromise us. We depend on continuing a poisonous, addictive relationship to the planet. Oil is our blood and our addiction compromises the Earth.

There is this amazing scene in the presidential vampire thriller *Blood Oath* by Christopher Farnsworth, the first in a series. The books are by no means perfect. Nathaniel Cade is a vampire secret agent sworn to protect every U.S. president since 1867. He is much less human than Bill Compton of *True Blood* or Edward Cullen of *Twilight* or Stefan of *The Vampire Diaries*. His view of the world is cynical; he sees himself above petty human foibles. Yet, in one surprising scene, he is standing in the back of an AA meeting. Cade never gives his name during the meetings; he never speaks, but he regards himself as an addict who once killed his best friend in blind bloodlust. He seeks a kind of solace and support from these meetings. Like Edward Cullen, he sticks to animal blood for his nourishment, but he never loses his desire and thirst for human blood. Religious, he wears a cross, which is painful, as a constant reminder. He is a kind of stand-in for our own addictions.

When I first thought about these desperately-struggling-to-be-moral vampires in literature and on television, I assumed it all started with the vampires I mentioned. But it probably goes back more than forty years, to before the Vampire Chronicles by Anne Rice. One of the first truly conflicted vampires might well be Barnabas in *Dark Shadows,* alternately murderous and moral. *Dark Shadows* started in 1966, but Barnabas didn't enter the story until 1967, just after the time Stewart Brand was sending out those buttons about seeing the Earth from space. In fact the word "vampire" was not used to describe Barnabas until 1968, just around the time we would see that first image from Apollo.

On December 24, 1968, Apollo 8 brought us that first good picture of our white and blue, fragile Earth as seen from space. The photograph was taken by astronaut William Anders. Apollo 8 was the first spaceflight with humans aboard to leave Earth's orbit, and the first really good color picture of the Earth was taken on that mission. On Christmas Day, 1968, when the astronauts were *still* on their mission, the *New York Times* ran an essay by poet Archibald MacLeish, "Riders on Earth Together, Brothers in Eternal Cold." He wrote that when people thought the Earth was "the World," they saw themselves as creatures at the center of the universe, "and from that high place they ruled and conquered as they pleased." Later, when science proved that the Earth was a minor star off at the edge of an "inconsiderable galaxy," people began to see themselves as helpless victims of a "senseless farce." But in the last few hours, he noted, the notion may have changed again, seeing the Earth as "whole and round and beautiful and small . . . " He ends with this:

> The medieval notion of the earth put man at the center of everything. The nuclear notion of the earth put him nowhere— beyond the range of reason even—lost in absurdity and war. This latest notion may have other consequences. Formed as it was in the minds of heroic voyagers who were also men, it may remake our image of mankind. . . .
>
> To see the earth as it truly is, small and blue and beautiful in that eternal silence where it floats, is to see ourselves as riders on the earth together, brothers on that bright loveliness in the eternal cold—brothers who know now they are truly brothers.

Rusty Schweickart, one of the astronauts on the next Apollo—Apollo 9—has said that the astronauts had so many checklists and tests to perform while up in space that there was little time for reflection. Like many astronauts, he looked at the continents from above and realized all the boundaries were artificial, and that the Earth was a whole. But when one of his fellow astronauts landed on the moon in Apollo 11, Schweickart described the experience this way in a 1974 essay:

> And now he looks back and he sees the Earth not as something big, where he can see the beautiful details, but now he sees the Earth as a small thing out there. And the contrast between that bright blue and white Christmas tree ornament and the black sky, that infinite universe, really comes through, and the size of it, the significance of it. It is so small and so fragile and such a precious little spot in that universe that you can block it out with your thumb. And you realize that on that small spot, that little blue and white thing, is everything that means anything to you—all of history and music and poetry and art and death and birth and love, tears, joy, games, all of it on that little spot out there that you can cover with your thumb. And you realize from that perspective that you've changed, that there's something new there, that the relationship is no longer what it was.

And he writes that he came to realize that being an astronaut did not make him special; he was simply a "sensing element" for humankind. The experience was not "his," he writes.

"It's you, it's we. It's life that's had that experience."

Quite simply, these images transformed the way we saw the Earth. For many of us, it was the first real understanding of ourselves as beings connected to the fate of the planet, who had a role in preserving it. Space seemed vast; our planet seemed small and vulnerable. What we did suddenly mattered.

This shift helped fuel the environmental movement. Soon after, in April 1970, the first Earth Day took place. Denis Hayes says in the film *Earth Days,* "We suddenly realized that the Earth was a very small thing. Much as if you live on an island you are much more acutely aware of the limitations of your resources and on your ability to pollute. That photograph of the Earth in this vast sea of space did pretty much the same thing for the whole planet."

The photographs from Apollo also showed the impact of oceans and weather and even human activities. We suddenly saw the Earth as a living system.

Although I have been a friend of Rusty Schweickart for decades and had heard his stories many times, and also had a copy of the first *Whole Earth Catalog,* and thought about those images of Earth for many years, it wasn't until I was almost done with this project and had put in the quotes above that I came across a remarkable book about all those images: *Earthrise* by Robert Poole. Poole notes that Anders, who took the Earthrise photograph, told a reporter, some twenty years later, the photograph was an afterthought for NASA, but when he thinks back to that voyage, "it was that Earth really stuck in my mind . . . it was a surprise. We didn't think about that." Poole notes that many people in the space program and, of course, science fiction writers, were, in his words, "astrofuturists," people who saw the Earth as the womb from which humanity would necessarily go forth and who argued that eventually Earth would have to be left behind, that it was a prison. Arthur C. Clarke made this argument, for example. My late husband would probably fall into this "astrofuturist" category. But the images from Apollo were so evocative that, in the end, they brought people's attention back to Earth.

It's very easy to romanticize this idea: that the image of the Earth from space allowed us to see that now we are brothers and sisters, boundaries are illusions, we all have to get along. But the deeper truth about this shift in perspective is a darker vision. Many of us began to see ourselves as morally compromised beings, unable to shift our lives to mirror the changes we viscerally understood—from this new perspective—to be necessary. So it wasn't the optimistic view—we are all brothers—of Archibald MacLeish. Our new sense of responsibility established a feeling of conflict and guilt.

Near the end of *Earthrise,* Poole quotes the late scientist Carl Sagan from a book called *Pale Blue Dot*:

> Our posturings, our imagined self-importance, the delusion that we have some privileged position, are challenged by this point of pale light. Our planet is a lonely speck in the great enveloping cosmic dark. . . . There is no hint that help will come from elsewhere to save us from ourselves.

You can see this change in perspective in the writings of Stewart Brand. When he put out the first edition of *The Whole Earth Catalog,* in 1968, right around the time of the image of Earthrise, there was a sense of incredible optimism. "We are as gods and might as well get good at it," are the opening words of the *Catalog.* But today, there's more of a sense of desperation about our role, and the shrinking amount of time we have to get it right. Brand's recent book, *Whole Earth Discipline,* changes the quote. It begins with the words: "We are as gods and HAVE to get good at it." What has partly led to our identification with vampires and the creation of vampires who are in a desperate moral struggle is the fear that our actions are causing irreversible damage.

But if vampires represent our own moral struggles, and if there is a growing sense of pessimism about our future at the moment, there's something else surprising going on. At the beginning of my own obsessive journey, as I wrestled with issues of mortality, power, persecution, and morality, it never occurred to me that this was also a spiritual voyage.

SPIRITUALITY

IN THE EARLY '70s, when I was just starting my radio show *Hour of the Wolf* on WBAI-FM, I came across a quotation from John Muir that is still one of my favorites: "When we try to pick out anything by itself, we find it hitched to everything else in the universe." A few years before I started the show, I was beginning to read a lot of environmental literature—Henry David Thoreau, John Muir, René Dubos, Loren Eiseley, Rachel Carson—and poetry like the "Smokey the Bear Sutra" by the poet Gary Snyder. And there was this notion, so elegantly expressed in the John Muir quote, that we were all ecstatically connected to the cosmos. Everything was interconnected. Remember, this was only a short time after the first Earth Day, and only a couple of years from that first image of the Earth from space. I began to believe that ecology was not only a political movement, but also a spiritual one, involving moral and ethical responsibility.

Bron Taylor has written a wonderful book called *Dark Green Religion*. And I think when I heard that Muir quotation back in the early 1970s, I had one of those moments Taylor might call a dark green religious moment. In *Dark Green Religion,* a term he coins, Taylor examines the spiritual views of environmentalists, surfers, and artists. Although he notes that ideas of sustainability and what one might call "green spirituality" have been adopted by many political groups, from Amnesty International to Greenpeace, *Dark Green Religion* is different in that it values a sacred whole more than the rights of individuals. He uses the word "dark" partly because these views are seen as dangerous by some and as salvation by others. It's also "dark" because of the passions it arouses, as seen in movements like Deep Ecology, and, possibly, because it does have a shadow side, which can lead to the violence of Earth liberation movements and extremists like the Unabomber.

Taylor defines "dark green religion" as a set of beliefs and practices with a central conviction that "nature is sacred, has intrinsic value, and is therefore due reverent care," as well as a belief in the interconnectedness and interdependent nature of life on Earth. He divides dark green religion into four types, which, taken together, include many different types of people: from atheists to animists to pantheists. They include people who see their religion as a metaphor and others who feel animals have souls and that there is an intelligence animating the universe. He includes people like Jane Goodall, Alice Walker, Charles Darwin, Al Gore, and Julia Butterfly Hill (who lived in a redwood tree for more than two years to prevent it from being cut down) and groups like Earth First! and the Animal Liberation Front. He even looks at films like *Avatar* and *The Lion King*. It was partly this kind of dark green religious moment that brought me into Paganism, although Taylor's book does not spend much time on contemporary Pagan religions.

So we come to 2012. I had already read some 230 vampire novels, not to mention a host of scholarly works, including Nina

Auerbach's *Our Vampires, Ourselves.* I had thought about power and its abuses, the rebellious outsider as hero, issues of mortality and the fate of the planet, but somehow I had left religion out of the picture. This was an odd omission since—although I come from a very secular family and upbringing—I have been a practicing Wiccan and Pagan since 1972. I have also been a journalist who has chronicled the contemporary Pagan spirituality movement for more than thirty years in the various editions of *Drawing Down the Moon: Witches, Druids, Goddess-Worshippers, and Other Pagans in America Today.* Despite all this, when I thought of why vampires have traction in our current culture, I did not think of the vampire as a symbol of spiritual transformation, and certainly not a positive one.

I entered into Paganism because of a love of ritual and a love of the Greek goddesses going back to childhood. And if I go back to my earliest dreams and fantasies of Paganism—the Greek goddesses that I so loved when I was twelve—I knew in the depths of my being that I didn't want to worship them; I wanted to *be* them. Probably not so different from the fantasies of becoming a vampire described in Riccardo's *Liquid Dreams of Vampires.* The goddesses became the stuff of fantasy, with me taking the role of Athena or Artemis in countless daydreams. Now this shouldn't seem so strange. The gods of old are still the stuff of countless childhood fantasies. After all, the Percy Jackson and the Olympians series by Rick Riordan is a current best-seller. There are actual day camps for kids based on the books, places where kids can go on all kinds of fantasy quests. I even visited one of them in Prospect Park in Brooklyn. But I was having my own childhood fantasies in the

1950s, and there were not many strong images of women when I was growing up. Artemis and Athena were about as good as it got. In 1958, at the age of twelve, I entered the world of ancient Greece as if it were my true homeland. Even years later when I would hear those old Olympic Airways ads with the slogan "Come home to Greece," I would think, *That is my homeland,* even though it took me until the 1980s to actually get there.

A year and a half later, when I was fourteen, during a horrible summer right after my parent's divorce, I was thrown into the arms of a difficult, wealthy New York family, the parents of a schoolmate. My mother didn't know what to do with me, and she thought that putting me in the hands of a wealthy family that was going on a long European vacation would be just the ticket. It was an extraordinary but lonely summer.

One night, I remember walking down the steps of the Roman Forum—something you can't do anymore at night. I remember taking off my shoes and feeling the stones on my bare feet, stones that countless Roman citizens and slaves had walked on some two thousand years ago. I remember feeling little jolts of electricity coursing through my feet, and I daydreamed that I was the goddess Athena who had come back down to Earth. I walked down the steps in the moonlight, fantasizing myself in that role.

I even wrote down in my diary imaginary conversations between my friend and me, with me taking the role of Athena. The other day, as I was thinking about how teens need to create heroic figures, and become them in fantasy and play, I went and found the old diary written in the summer of 1960, when I was fourteen. I admit total embarrassment—even today—when I read the passages. At the time I wrote the diary I certainly felt that anyone who admits to such fantasies belongs in a mental institution. Perhaps these fantasy conversations allowed me to feel more powerful in a very vulnerable and powerless situation.

Some time before college these fantasies ended. After all, no one believed in the Greek gods, and only crazy people pretended to *be* them. Many years later, when I discovered the contemporary and revived nature religions and Paganism, I was given a tape of a ritual recorded in England. A man read an invocation: "Here ye the words of the Great Mother who was of old, also called Artemis, Astarte . . . " and he listed the names of all those goddesses I had been attracted to at the age of twelve and thirteen. And then the woman on the tape began to speak in beautiful poetry, taking the role of the goddess. "I, who am the beauty of the green earth, and the white moon among the stars, and the mystery of the waters, I call your soul to arise and come unto me, for I am the soul of nature who giveth life to the universe . . . " You could hear Brahms in the background. I listened to this woman, an adult with a British accent, speaking as the goddess in a ritual, and she wasn't crazy; she wasn't in a mental hospital. I remember feeling waves of relief, beginning to sob, feeling for once that my own fantasies and dreams were—oh my god—even possibly normal, and that there was a path to open the drawer of dreams, aspirations, and spiritual questing that I had closed in my teenage years. I realized I could allow those feelings to come again into my life. It was the beginning of my Pagan journey.

Now, you could argue that there is something narcissistic about all these fantasies about being a goddess or a superhero. What good does it do, you may ask. Does it have anything to do with real power, with being more confident, resilient, and more able to be active in the world? I would say you have to be very careful, but perhaps, yes. Take this story.

With the exception of one stint selling housewares at Bloomingdale's, almost every job I have had has been in the nonprofit sector. Those who have worked for decades at nonprofits, particularly women, are often people who have trouble asking for money. The joke goes, "I should pay them for working here!" Among other things, it's due partly to a lack of confidence and to the long history of women not being paid as well as men. So, I had been working in public radio for about ten years when I came up for my first real job at NPR. I had been a newscaster, a job that paid $85 a week; I had been a producer, a job that paid $160 a week, but now I was going to a larger and more prosperous company, NPR. It was 1979. After I was told that I had gotten the job, a very good male friend who worked at NPR gave me some advice. "When you negotiate salary, tell them you want $25,000 a year. They will say $20,000, and you will end up with a salary of about $23,000." It was clearly very sound advice from someone on the inside. So I walked into the office of the person who was doing the hiring, in fact, the head of news at NPR, and when we came to the salary issue, she said, "How about twenty?" And guess what I said? I said. "Sure." I didn't even make the smallest attempt to negotiate.

Now fast-forward about ten years. I am up for another position, and it's time to negotiate salary. And I know myself; I know my tendencies, my need to please, my need to be loved and to be seen as a team player. So what do I do? I write the word "Athena" on some paper on my desk. I do what people in the magical and prayerful world often call an affirmation. I close my eyes and enter a more meditative state and say something like this: "There is a creative power in the universe that some call God, some call light or energy, and I choose to call Goddess. This power is all around us, and I, in microcosm, embody this power as well. I draw to myself these powers and abilities—the strength I need to ask for what I need, the powers of attention, concentration, the right words at the right time, confidence, a spirit of generosity and humor. I draw the power of Athena and her wisdom and strength to me. I also dissolve and release all the things that would hinder me in this effort: fear, confusion, and self-doubt. And all this happens for the good of all, and so it is." (By the way, if you like this form of affirmation, *Positive Magic,* by the late Marion Weinstein, is the book for you.)

I do this for five to seven minutes before my interview takes place, and when I go into the interview I am absolutely focused. I know exactly what I want and need. I feel strong, confident, and relaxed. And in fact, all goes the way I want it, at least as far as the negotiation.

Now, that does not mean that I have that kind of strength two hours later, or that I feel in any way like the goddess Athena by the next day. All my own doubts, and my feelings of powerlessness, return in time. But the images, the fantasies, the words, all of them can be used as a tactic, a way to give myself confidence in a real situation. In fact, I admit that I do a tiny version of this before I give a lecture or appear on a radio or television show. These kinds of affirmations can be very powerful psychological tools to help you access deeper parts of yourself as you put yourself forward in the world.

Recently, I came across a book that suddenly brought these notions to the fore and connected them to vampires. The book is called *Gothicka: Vampire Heroes, Human Gods, and the New Supernatural* (2012), by Victoria Nelson, a professor at Goddard College. As I began to read, I realized that in many ways Nelson and I were on the same wavelength, although she hadn't mentioned ecology, and I, up to this point, hadn't mentioned religion.

Here's what Nelson argues. She says that in the 21st century, the supernatural has taken a "surprising new turn toward the light." Although still accessed through the grotesque and monstrous, it is, she says, "showing signs of outgrowing the dark supernaturalism it inherited from its eighteenth-century ancestor." Most relevant, she sees it as a vehicle for new religious movements.

She notes the many religious and magical groups that have the idea of incarnating as gods on Earth. She notes how magical groups aim to develop will, attention, and imagination as a way of projecting themselves into another dimension to become "a kind of divinity." She even believes that in our time, "for those outside the pale of orthodoxy, Gothick pop culture products such as the Great Old Ones, vampires, Klingons, and orcs offer the only easily accessible bridge to the transcendental."

Eventually she takes on *Twilight,* in one of the most fascinating analyses I have seen. Remember, I argued for a class analysis of The Twilight Saga—Bella as a middle-class girl living in a boring family situation, attracted to two large extended families, one tribal and working class, the other upper class and educated. I argued that the Mormon influence on the series is not abstinence or anti-feminism, but more the appeal of large families. But Nelson says that if there is a Mormon element in Meyer's writing, it is the belief that if you live the right life, you will die and become a kind of god. Think about all those ideas about Mormons getting their own planet in the afterlife! In a chapter called "The Bright God Beckons," with a picture of Edward Cullen sparkling in the light like some kind of tantric deity, Nelson notes that, when turned, Bella becomes a perfected being; she is transformed into a kind of goddess. She becomes someone totally empowered and a total equal with Edward Cullen. Nelson quotes Bella in *Twilight* saying that she doesn't always want to be Lois Lane: "I want to be Superman too." Nelson gives many other examples from vampire fiction of a human protagonist whose supernatural change—sometimes into a vampire, sometimes not—leads to becoming a divinity of sorts. Think of how Anita Blake in Laurell K. Hamilton's later novels takes on more and more of the powers of the beings she once hunted.

It's just like that old quote from Stewart Brand's first *Whole Earth Catalog*, "We are as gods and might as well get good at it." Looking at *Twilight*, Nelson notes how the vampire "portrayed for two hundred years as a ruthless unredeemed killer [has turned] into the ethical, committed lover of a heroine whose fate is to find her true identity by dying and triumphantly joining him on a transformed dark side." Transformed into light.

The theme of so many of these books and movies, she argues, is spiritual transcendence. At the end of *Gothicka*, Nelson asks why this is the spiritual quest of the moment. "Why," she wonders, is this about human gods, "and not a set of new invented deities?" She doesn't have an answer. But she does note that, like the Athena fantasy of my childhood, the *Twilight* fans do not want to worship the vampire goddess Bella Swan or simply fall into Edward's arms; they want to *be* her or him. "The notion of self-deification is somehow in the metaphysical air surrounding all these various narratives," Nelson says. And she is optimistic that many of these beliefs, although individualistic, are anti-authoritarian and turn away from the demonic and move toward human accountability. The conflicted protagonists win the moral struggles by being humans first, supernaturals only second. And I would note that some of them, like Buffy, give up their own power for the power of all.

Katherine Ramsland, the biographer of Anne Rice, spent an enormous amount of time, like Riccardo, talking with people who wanted to *be* vampires. She also comes to the conclusion that vampires are now more a shadow of ourselves than something out there and that their powers make them "like gods of ancient times." She says vampires have "a radiance erotically reminiscent of a supreme being," and that young people often see themselves as "fragile and flickering . . . " They are exactly the opposite of the strong, long-lived vampire. In a world where corporations are people and individual action often seems meaningless, in a world where young people need, to quote Rice yet again, "a noble path through the hideous passage that Western Culture has set up for them," desiring, fantasizing, and using various spiritual techniques to gain more personal power seems a pretty simple and obvious path to take.

Of course, there is one problem: self-delusion. Everyone knows that those on spiritual quests are vulnerable. So many people on these kinds of journeys come to think that they have *the* answer, not simply one of many answers. You have to be grounded, and have a mature sense of self, to use the tools of fantasy without believing in their "reality," without being sucked into some crazy belief that these are more than strategies and tools in your own voyage of self-discovery. Many have lost their way. Gurus and magical practitioners who have gone off track litter the pathways.

So as I continue to watch and identify with those conflicted, desperately-struggling-to-be-moral vampires, I note that my own search for spiritual transformation has merged with wanting an answer to the urgent questions of planetary survival that face us all. It is no longer enough to fantasize, even if it helps. As Brand would later say, "We are as gods and HAVE to get good at it." We need to find our voice as powerful activists. But we can use every fantasy, every dream, and every imaginative tool we can obtain in our toolbox. Even vampires.

And one last thing. As I have taken this journey, many people have looked at me askance and have silently thought, *How could an intelligent person like you spend* four years *reading such crap?* Here's my answer. I use a quote I found in Nelson's *Gothicka*; she says it's in the spirit of the late, great science fiction writer Philip K. Dick: "When the divine has been exiled from the table of serious art and intellectual discussion for well over a century, you have to look for it in what elite culture thinks of as the trash."

PART TWO

Margot's Annotated Bibliography of Vampire Fiction

An overview of more than 270 novels, as well as anthologies, short stories, and assorted nonfiction.

When people hear that I have read some 270 vampire novels, they often say, "There can't be 270 vampire novels!" In fact, according to a bibliography in *The Vampire Archives* (2009), as of that date there were more than five thousand novels and short stories. By now there are, of course, a whole lot more. But the strange and wonderful thing about vampire stories is that they traverse every genre. That actually makes sense when you think about it, because adults, teens, whites, blacks, gays, straights, old, young, everyone is exploring the themes that vampire stories take on: power, morality, death, sex, identity, spiritual transformation, and the plight of the planet. You can explore all these themes in vampire stories.

Vampire fiction is all over the map, from detective stories to romance, from alternate history to science fiction, from comedy to horror to probes of serious issues, from true literary treasures to total fluff, from tales about geeky, nerdy teen vampires to the stereotypical stories of vampires that are gorgeous and sultry with perfect bodies. Steven Moore writes in *The Vampire in Verse: An Anthology*, "The Vampire is a mirror into our secret self," so it isn't surprising that vampire novels touch every genre. The more than 270 novels described here are not necessarily the best. They were just the ones that fell into my hands during a four-year obsession.

If you prefer to read only a specific genre, skim to the types of literature that interest you. You may be surprised that vampires populate some of the types of literature you love. I list some of my favorite novels and series at the very end. As I said, I've had fun reading these books.

Let's look at "genre." Despite a few examples of speculative literature that reviewers usually do not deign to call science fiction or fantasy—I am thinking about works by Doris Lessing and Margaret Atwood among others—we still live in a world where science fiction and fantasy, and most genre literature, certainly romance, is denigrated, even though more than 20 percent of books sold yearly fall into the romance category.

Ursula Le Guin, who wrote two science fiction novels that deserve a place in any literary canon, *The Left Hand of Darkness* and *The Dispossessed,* wrote in the introduction to the 1989 edition of *The Language of the Night: Essays on Fantasy and Science Fiction,* "The Canoneers of Literature still refuse to admit that genrification is a political tactic and that the type of fiction they distinguish as serious, mainstream, literary, etc., is itself a genre without inherent superiority to any other."

In her 1972 National Book Award acceptance speech, she says that realism is "perhaps the least adequate means of understanding or portraying the incredible realities of our existence." And in a 1971 interview in a fanzine, when asked why she writes science fiction, Le Guin answers, "I write science fiction because that is what publishers call my books. Left to myself, I should call them novels."

All the books and short stories listed here are in some way fantasy or speculative fiction. After all, we are talking about vampires and except for the tiny number of people who actually drink blood and claim to be vampires, we are talking about something from dreams, myth, folklore, science fiction, or fantasy. So, it begs the question, why is fantasy important? And why is there this hard division between those who are riveted by speculative fiction of all kinds and others who find it a lower form of literature they would never pick up? It clearly has nothing to do with intelligence.

For me, science fiction and fantasy are a way to re-imagine everything without the blinders and constraints of our present culture. Robert Anton Wilson, who, along with Robert Shea, wrote *The Illuminatus! Trilogy*, once told an interviewer, "We can't even visualize the size of the local galaxy except in certain high states." What I have always loved about science fiction is the way it allows you to rethink all social relations: work, marriage, death, politics, even architecture. There is one scene in Ursula Le Guin's extraordinary novel *The Dispossessed* in which the protagonist, who comes from a more gently anarchist world, notices the way chairs are designed in our society, with an odd, and to his mind, uncomfortable sexuality. This becomes an opportunity to rethink architecture and sensuality in ways that would be difficult outside of such a book. By getting away from the constraints of "reality," one is free to imagine broader and deeper and even to see the world as it is with more clarity.

My late husband, John Gliedman, who must have read at least a thousand science fiction novels during his life, said that we human beings are limited by our very success as a species. We really don't know how other smart species get along in the universe, assuming they are there, and assuming we could meet them and survive the encounter or even get a chance to examine their artifacts. He believed the real reason for venturing into space and attempting to contact alien civilizations—if they exist—is to expand the mind and the imagination, to figure out how to get beyond the limits of our environment and the way we have evolved over millions of years. After all, on Earth there is only one basic pattern for organizing life forms, using DNA. "Think of what it would be to discover life forms that are organized differently," he told a panel at the Conference on World Affairs, in Boulder, Colorado. "We suffer from the sample size problem. It would be nice to stop just looking at ourselves in the mirror and meet some of the stuff out there."

Margaret L. Carter, in her book *Different Blood: The Vampire as Alien,* uses the term "alien" in the science fiction sense, as alien species, not as outsider. Her book analyzes the countless novels and short stories where vampires are depicted as a separate species, as opposed to some kind of supernatural demon. These novels range from Whitley Strieber's *The Hunger* to Michael Talbot's *The Delicate Dependency* to Octavia Butler's *Fledgling.* Carter says something very similar to John; she takes the title of her book from a quote from *Out of the Silent Planet,* the first book in C. S. Lewis's science fiction or space trilogy. The protagonist, Ransom, is conversing with an alien who is surprised to learn that Ransom comes from a planet with only one seemingly truly intelligent species. The alien says, "Your thought must be at the mercy of your blood . . . you cannot compare it with thought that floats on a different blood." It's the same idea: we humans are limited because we have only ourselves to see in the mirror. Science fiction is an attempt to give us those different bloods or perspectives, to fill in for that limitation of having no other species with which to compare ourselves.

And yet, there is a kind of Calvinist disapproval of fantasy and speculative fiction in our society; we either fear it or dislike it as inferior. This is particularly true of elites who dismiss it as low art. In Le Guin's essay "Why Are Americans Afraid of Dragons?", you could easily substitute vampires. She writes that fantasy is true: "It isn't factual, but it is true. Children know that. Adults know it too, and that is precisely why many of them are afraid of fantasy. They know that its truth challenges, even threatens, all that is false, all that is phony, unnecessary, and trivial in the life they have let themselves be forced into living. They are afraid of dragons, because they are afraid of freedom."

Many issues of politics, philosophy, and certainly spiritual transformation are often eschewed by the literary elite and are often not seen as fit subjects for novels. As you begin looking at this survey, really an annotated list of novels as well as some short stories and nonfiction books, you might ponder again the quote at the end of Part One, the quote by Victoria Nelson in her book *Gothicka*: "When the divine has been exiled from the table of serious art and intellectual discussion for well over a century, you have to look for it in what elite culture thinks of as the trash."

Remember that within each genre, quality and depth of ideas vary widely. For example, take romance, which runs the gamut from beautifully written to really awful, formulaic soft porn. I recently read *Dark Prince,* the first of the Dark Series by Christine Feehan. Feehan has written more than forty books in the last twelve years, and more than twenty in the Dark Series. I barely got through the first novel; there were so many bad, repetitive sex scenes, more than a dozen in one novel, that I vowed I would never open one of her books again. But if you look at the Argeneau Vampire series, by Lynsay Sands, there are also several formulaic sex scenes per novel, but there is a Jane Austen quality to the books that I find charming: the mother of a Canadian vampire family is eager to marry off each of her children, one for each novel. It's fairly light, fluffy, and comedic, but I read the first nine novels with a kind of guilty pleasure. Then you get romance novels with poetic writing and complex relationships. *The Circle Trilogy*, by Nora Roberts, would be my nomination for something in the romance category that is superbly done. One last caveat: many of these novels fit in several categories, and my choice of where to put them is, at times, totally arbitrary. With that in mind, let's begin this survey of vampire literature genre by genre.

DETECTIVE VAMPIRE FICTION

Authors:

Tanya Huff, Charlie Huston, Trevor O. Munson, Barbara Hambly,
Fred Saberhagen, P. N. Elrod, Jim Butcher, Fred Vargas,
Mel Nicolai and Jana Perinchief, Jennifer Rardin, Jeaniene Frost

THE VAMPIRE DETECTIVE NOVELS I have read range from classic hard boiled, to supernatural investigation. In most of the books, but not all, the vampire is the detective. He or she can be everything from tough talking Joe Pitt in the five wonderful noir novels that take place in an almost believable dystopian New York, to the suave and romantic Henry Fitzroy in the Tanya Huff Blood Books series about Canadian private investigator Victoria Nelson.

The Blood Books, by Tanya Huff. This series comprises five novels that were made into a two season Lifetime TV series. They are *Blood Price, Blood Trail, Blood Lines, Blood Pact,* and *Blood Debt.* There is also a short story collection titled *Blood Bank.* Victoria Nelson is a former cop, compelled to leave the force because of deteriorating eyesight. She becomes a private investigator in Toronto and often teams up with a cop on the force,

Detective Celluci. Celluci is clearly attracted to Nelson, but little is expressed openly. Nelson also teams up with Henry Fitzroy, a four-hundred-year-old vampire who is the bastard son of King Henry VIII. He is a romance writer in the books and a graphic novelist in the TV series. The unresolved tension between the three characters is at the heart of the books and the best aspect of the television show. The three of them solve crimes, almost always with a supernatural twist. Huff also wrote three novels about Fitzroy and his sometime male lover. They take place in Vancouver and are not nearly as successful: *Smoke and Shadows, Smoke and Mirrors, Smoke and Ashes.*

The Joe Pitt Casebooks series, by Charlie Huston. This series takes place in a dark and dystopian New York City. Again, there are five novels: *Already Dead, No Dominion, Half the Blood of Brooklyn, Every Last Drop,* and *My Dead Body.* Vampire gangs divide New York. There is the Coalition, the strongest group; the Society, which seems like a group of aging vampire hippies; the Enclave, a group of vampires who starve themselves in an attempt to achieve enlightenment; and many other smaller vampire groups that have their own territories. Most regular humans go about their lives totally unaware of this dark underbelly of the city. Joe Pitt is trying to live an independent life as a PI—not beholden to either the Coalition or the Society. He has relations with both groups and gets in trouble with both. He drinks blood mostly by buying it or getting it as a reward for work, but he occasionally taps people. He cannot be in the sun, but he can be awake in the daytime. Pitt's world is dark and violent. He is in love with a human, who doesn't know his true nature in the first few books. By the second book, *No Dominion,* you realize that Huston "gets" New York. There are wonderful scenes in Alphabet City and on the A train. One book takes place mostly in Brooklyn, another in the Bronx. Pitt often has to make compromises and imperfect choices. This is a violent world filled with blood and gore. The writing is spare and minimalist, but Pitt comes off well, and the dark vision of a future New York City is totally believable to this New Yorker. I list this series among my favorites in "The Best" section.

***Angel of Vengeance,* by Trevor O. Munson.** This is the book that inspired the CBS series *Moonlight,* but the book is much darker. Munson says he read *Dracula* and followed it with a Raymond Chandler novel; he decided to create a bloodsucking Philip Marlowe, and he has. Michael Angel, who becomes the much sweeter and romantic Mick St. John in *Moonlight,* treats his bloodlust like an addiction; he was a heroin addict previously and he uses needles to mainline blood. He sleeps in a freezer (as in *Moonlight*) because the vampires in this world rot, just much more slowly, and he can't glamour people unless he is invited in. Stakes paralyze; burning kills, but you have to scatter the ashes as Angel learns a bit too late. The story involves vampires, drug dealers, a love interest from the 1940s, and vengeance from long ago. The character of Mick St. John in the TV show is more complex and far more attractive than Michael Angel in the book. There are almost no good guys in this novel, but Angel does have rules: don't kill women, children, or innocents. Munson couldn't get this book published until after he worked on the television series.

Those Who Hunt the Night, **by Barbara Hambly.** Hambly's *Those Who Hunt the Night* has a very Sherlock Holmes quality. Set in 1907, at the turn of the century, someone is killing the vampires of London. The oldest vampire, Simon Ysidro, seeks the help of a former British spy, James Asher. Asher and his wife Lydia, a doctor, investigate the vampire world, eventually going to Paris to seek out the oldest of all vampires.

The Holmes-Dracula File, **by Fred Saberhagen.** Saberhagen decided to turn the Dracula mythos on its head and make him the good guy. This book is part of a series of books that do just that. In this novel Dracula meets up with Sherlock Holmes and, at times, it almost feels like a Sherlock Holmes novel; it is told partly in the voice of Watson and partly in the voice of Dracula, who wakes up as an imprisoned experimental subject in a nefarious plot to bring the plague to London during the Queen's jubilee. Dracula escapes and Holmes investigates the disappearance of a medical researcher in Sumatra. The two plots come together quite well.

The Vampire Files, by P. N. Elrod. P. N. Elrod has written a dozen vampire detective novels called the Vampire Files. I read the first six: *Bloodlist, Lifeblood, Bloodcircle, Art in the Blood, Fire in the Blood,* and *Blood on the Water.* The novels take place in the 1930s in Chicago and revolve around two private investigators: an Englishman named Charles Escott and Jack Fleming, a former New York journalist who has recently become a vampire. The first two novels involve Fleming's search for the woman who turned him. The books are not brilliant; they do improve as they go along.

Jack Fleming is not very reflective, although he becomes more concerned about his condition in later books, and that makes the novels somewhat more interesting. Elrod has never lived in Chicago. She told me she wrote the books with lots of research and Google maps. For that reason there isn't the kind of authentic Chicago flavor you will find in, say, the Chicagoland Vampires series (see Regional Vampire Novels).

The Dresden Files, by Jim Butcher. Jim Butcher has written a whole series of novels, the Dresden Files. They are not specifically about vampires. Harry Dresden is a wizard who works with the police department to solve magical crimes. He also takes his own clients. In the first book, *Storm Front,* he is called in to solve a horrific murder, but he comes under suspicion by the White Council, which oversees the magical realm because he did something "black" in the past. Harry is a loner, who almost never trusts anyone. The first book has few vampires, only a terrifying demon vampire, Bianca, who runs an escort service. Because of his magical abilities, Dresden can see the demon reality beneath her gorgeous exterior, earning her enmity forever. Dresden does face moral dilemmas, resisting the lure of the dark side. I skipped to book six, *Blood Rites,* because the reviews said it had a vampire theme. *Blood Rites* has three types of vampires. The Black Court is demonic; they react to all the gothic symbols: crosses, garlic, holy water, etc. They are monstrous and bestial. I haven't quite understood the Red Court yet. The main focus of *Blood Rites* is the White Court; they are energy vampires, succubae, who feed on sexual energy and become an object of desire for humans. It is a moral quagmire, because eventually the energy loss is too much and the prey will die. Thomas of the Raith family is such a vampire, but he has fallen in love with his prey, Justine. In the end, he almost kills her and she is a ghost of her former self. Yet he is basically a lovely guy who wants freedom from this curse for his sister Inari, who has not even learned what she is, or could become. Lara, the other sister, is a total seductress, and the father of the family is deeply evil. Dresden finds out that many of those who mentored him in the magical arts are more complex morally and less blameless than he thought. The book has a very good description of energy vampires.

An Uncertain Place, **by Fred Vargas.** Fred Vargas is the pseudonym for French female mystery writer Frédérique Audoin-Rouzeau, who has written a series of novels featuring Paris Commissioner Jean-Baptiste Adamsberg. Part of the book takes place in Serbia. Adamsberg is a fascinating character. He seems to be in a fog half the time but then has sudden moments of amazing intuition. Adamsberg is confronted with a series of grisly crimes. Seventeen shoes with feet in them are found in Highgate Cemetery. Two other bodies are found almost pulverized. Cutting feet off and pulverizing bodies turn out to be ways to kill vampires in folklore. There are no "real" vampires in this mystery, but there are those who act on their fears of vampires, using myth and folklore: for example, bodies not decomposing and sighs from the grave. The real story is a plot to destroy Adamsberg and a curse that goes back three hundred years.

The Shake, **by Mel Nicolai and Jana Perinchief.** Shake is a vampire who is about one hundred years old. He is trying to figure out if there is a moral way to decide whom to kill and whom to save. After killing a woman, he becomes obsessed with the mystery around her late husband's murder and a missing child. His search to unravel the mystery leads him to find his maker. The book is filled with philosophical musings. At one point the vampire says he wishes becoming a vampire had given him more clarity. Instead it just gave him speed, strength, and more time to stumble around. There are some interesting thoughts about power and the resistance of vampires to groups and group ideas. The first person narrative doesn't always work.

• • •

It's hard to know whether these next selections belong in the detective genre; they could more accurately be described as CIA thriller/romance novels. Often, a tough talking woman CIA agent teams up with a suave vampire to rid the world of evil. The Jaz Parks novels by Jennifer Rardin and the Night Huntress novels by Jeaniene Frost fall into this category.

Once Bitten, Twice Shy, **by Jennifer Rardin.** In the series opener to Rardin's Jaz Parks series, Vayl is a three-hundred-year-old vampire, and Jaz Parks is his new partner. A previous vampire killer, she is now a partner assassin for the CIA. She finds Vayl very attractive, and there is definitely a romantic tension between them, but it is left alone. The character of Vayl is drawn well; he often has a hard time navigating the modern world. There is a lot of sass and humor, and the book gets better as it goes along, but it's a pretty stock story. There is a terrorist plastic surgeon and a plague that could destroy the world. There are definitely evil vampires and other monsters. There is also some mystery about Jaz; she is subject to blackouts and was involved in a serious tragedy that killed most of her old team, including her loved one. The writing is only fair and there wasn't enough there to make me read on in the series.

The Night Huntress series, by Jeaniene Frost. In this series of novels, the word "grave" is in every title. I have read five novels in the series: *Halfway to the Grave, One Foot in the Grave, At Grave's End, Destined for an Early Grave,* and *This Side of the Grave.* Frost has written at least two other urban fantasy series, the Night Huntress World series and the Night Prince series. Cat, or Catherine Crawfield, is half vampire, half human. Her mother was raped by a newly turned vampire, so his sperm were still living, which is how she came to be born. Her mother thinks her daughter is evil and constantly worries that she will "turn" and start to drink blood. Cat becomes a vampire slayer, always looking for her evil dad while pretending to be an ordinary person. She is stronger than other humans, although not as strong as a vampire, and she doesn't have fangs, but her eyes occasionally flash green. In this world, the only way to kill a vampire is by a silver stake to the heart, or by beheading; many of the gothic rules do not apply: they like night, but they can stay awake, and can survive a little sunlight. Cat meets Bones, a vampire bounty hunter, who goes after certain evil vampires. They eventually team up and fall in love. Clandestine government agencies finally employ her, and she is forced to make tragic choices between her problematic mother and the love of her life. A satisfying read that definitely fits into the moral vampire genre.

In the second book Cat meets up with her rapist vampire father. Bones, her vampire lover, is a charming Brit, and there is a lot of hot sex and blood exchange between them. Frost doesn't reach the insanity of the later Anita Blake novels, but there is too much sex and violence for my taste and not many moral dilemmas. By book three, I grew increasingly tired of the torture, violence, and over-the-top sex. There is not much compassion. Compassion here often means a quick death as opposed to mind-numbing torture. Bones is getting to be boring: super sex, super powers, a jealous nature, and a British accent, and Cat is getting to be just too much of a killing machine. In book four, Cat has to decide whether or not to finally become a vampire, a decision that has unforeseen consequences. Her mother also is forced to undergo a change that takes the plot in unusual directions. By book five I had had enough, even though there is a lovely section where Cat finally breaks down an emotional wall and admits her vulnerabilities to Bones. But then it is back to killing ghouls again.

PRESIDENTIAL VAMPIRE THRILLERS

Authors:

Jeff Gillenkirk, Christopher Farnsworth, Seth Grahame-Smith

YOU WOULD NEVER THINK that there would be a whole category of novels devoted to vampires and politics, but it makes sense. Power is one of the main themes in vampire literature. Many vampire novels assume that the undead, with their long life and history, get heavily involved in political games. In fact, in Carrie Vaughn's Kitty Norville books, a series devoted to a werewolf with a midnight radio show, Norville comes across ancient vampires who are involved in "The Long Game," a kind of political gamesmanship that goes on for centuries. Vaughn does not write presidential thrillers, but several recent novelists do go there.

***Pursuit of Darkness,* by Jeff Gillenkirk.** My current favorite is Jeff Gillenkirk's *Pursuit of Darkness,* a perfect read before a presidential election. Gillenkirk was once a speechwriter for Mario Cuomo and he has an excellent grasp of Washington political culture. An alcoholic *Washington Post* reporter is moved off politics to a less prestigious beat but is given a new chance to write a profile of

Jonathan Drees, a powerful GOP political operative—think Karl Rove. Drees tells Nate Hallberg, the reporter, that he is really a two-hundred-year-old vampire, and he entices him with some data, but not enough to prove it. Hallberg realizes there are vampires in the halls of power and in the FBI, and games within games. They have their own agenda, which is keeping the world stable enough so there is always a good blood supply. There are real insights into the political machinations of D.C. politics and the clueless nature of much of the media. I list this title among my favorites in "The Best" section.

The President's Vampire series, by Christopher Farnsworth. Christopher Farnsworth has written three Nathaniel Cade novels, *Blood Oath, The President's Vampire,* and *Red, White, and Blood,* with more expected. Nathaniel Cade is a vampire who has been defending presidents since Andrew Johnson. He is a secret weapon and secret agent that each president and only certain handlers know about. He is somewhat jaundiced, on the surface, beyond feeling, strong and merciless, a kind of Jack Bauer character. What redeems *Blood Oath* is that Cade has some feelings and is almost an ascetic. He wears a cross, even though it hurts. He drinks animal blood and refuses human blood even though it would make him stronger, and he goes to AA meetings because he sees his own desire for human blood as an addiction. Bound to the current president, an Obama-like figure, Cade is a Christian who believes himself damned. Unemotional and inhuman, he is oath-bound and moral.

The second book, *The President's Vampire,* has flashbacks to 9/11, to President Kennedy's assassination, and other events in the past. Cade almost fails in this novel, which makes the story more interesting, since he is no longer totally superhuman. The threat is from the Shadow Company and an old nemesis. Unfortunately much of the evil is of the supernatural monster mode, with human beings turned into lizard-like creatures who become killing machines. Josh Barrow, Cade's handler, grows and becomes much more of an adult in this second book. But there are some false notes for those of us who were around in the 1960s, including the description of Robert Kennedy.

Book three, *Red, White, and Blood,* takes place only months, and then weeks, before the 2012 election. It features a supernatural monster called the Boogeyman, whom Cade has never been able to kill. I was becoming sick of the Cade novels—too many supernatural monsters and not enough character development—until two-thirds of the way through book three, when Cade finally drinks blood from a victim. There is a surprising ending and we finally see an emotional Cade, but it may be too little, too late.

Abraham Lincoln: Vampire Hunter, by Seth Grahame-Smith. This novel doesn't quite fall into the presidential thriller category, but close enough, and it's a lot better than the author's previous effort: *Pride and Prejudice and Zombies.* The premise is impossible: Abraham Lincoln's journal is found with details of a secret life as a vampire hunter. Abe watches his mother die and realizes she was killed by a vampire. He vows revenge. He is trained to kill vampires by a vampire hunter—who turns out to be a vampire himself, although a moral one. Lincoln finds that his first love also died from a vampire and one of his children as well. There's some nice speculation about the origin of vampires—are they demons or simply another species? And the best part is that evil vampires side with the South in the Civil War, since there is nothing like slavery to ensure a consistent blood supply. The war against slavery becomes a war against vampires, and the Emancipation Proclamation becomes another way to disarm the undead threat. But it's not all black and white; there are vampires on the Union side, like Henry, the mysterious vampire who trains Lincoln and gives the author Lincoln's secret journal. And there is a surprise ending. The film version is quite different from the book, with no knowledge of Henry's true identity until near the end. Both book and film end in modern times, but the movie simplifies and doesn't have vampires, other than Henry, fighting on the Union side. The ending of the book is more satisfying than the movie. Surprisingly, the novel works.

HORROR: VAMPIRES as PURE EVIL, or CLOSE TO IT

Authors:

Stephen King, Justin Cronin, Dan Simmons, Guillermo Del Toro and Chuck Hogan, John Ajvide Lindqvist, Poppy Z. Brite, Beck Sherman, Joyce Carol Oates

GIVEN THE THEMES I am playing with, vampires as pure evil with no moral struggle are not terribly interesting to me. But I am including a few here, either because they are famous works, with masterful writing, or they became recent best-sellers. In some cases the bloodsuckers are not even sentient, let alone questioning; in others, they are simply pure evil, a plague upon the land.

'Salem's Lot, by Stephen King. Perhaps the classic of this genre. I found it extremely scary. It took me more than a month to finish it; I stopped around page 200 and it took weeks for me to pick it up again. Second, as I have said, I don't really like gothic, totally evil vampires with no redemptive qualities. Ben Mears, an author, comes back to Jerusalem's Lot to write a book and exorcise a very bad memory about something he saw in an old house. The house is later bought by a vampire and his servant. These two come to town, open a furniture shop, and begin to turn the townspeople. Soon few humans are left. This is a crosses-and-holy-water vampire book. These items, wooden stakes, and fire are the only weapons that work. As with much of King, the writing is excellent. But I prefer a philosophically struggling vampire any time.

The Passage, **by Justin Cronin.** A 766-page summer blockbuster with a huge blurb from Stephen King. A secret military experiment goes awry, the disease gets out, it creates monsters, and the Earth is practically destroyed. The monsters are vampire-like in that they feed on blood; they don't speak and remain only a shadow of their former selves. Most were test subjects and former death row inmates. There is a certain hive mind to them. What makes *The Passage* an intense read are the adventures of a group of survivors determined to find the source of the plague destroying their world; they go out into the destroyed world fighting the "virals" or "smokes" or "jumps," various terms that different groups of survivors call the vampire-like monsters. There is also a mysterious girl who holds the key to discovering the truth of what happened. The plot carries you forward, and some of the writing is lyrical and poetic. One of the most interesting aspects of the novel is the new culture, language, and social organizations that the survivors create. This is the first of a trilogy, and movies are on the way. But by the end of the first book, Cronin has killed off most of the interesting characters, begging the question, why should we care?

Carrion Comfort, **by Dan Simmons.** Published in 1989, *Carrion Comfort* is considered one of the great horror novels. It is long and complex and is a totally different kind of vampire novel than any other I have read. In his extraordinary introduction to the twentieth-anniversary edition, Simmons, whose wonderful *Children of the Night* I review elsewhere, devotes more than twenty pages to his idea of mind vampires, those who control your will. There are no bloodsuckers here, no fangs, and only one character who uses his mind to impose sex on the unwilling. Bloodsuckers are not real, Simmons says, but few of us get through life without becoming prey to at least one mind vampire.

The story starts with a Holocaust survivor and psychiatrist, Dr. Saul Laski, who found himself victim to a mind vampire in the camps: Wilhelm Von Borchert, a Nazi *oberst* who later becomes a film producer in Hollywood. In one horrific scene, prisoners, including Laski, are human pieces in a chess board that turns into a blood and gore nightmare that Lewis Carroll could never have conceived. Three of those with what they call "the Ability" have banded together—Wilhelm, now called Willi Borden, Nina Drayton, and Melanie Fuller. Once a year they gather for "The Game," which involves controlling various people and changing events though mind control. Who wins depends on what changes have taken place and whom they have killed over the past year. For example, one of the three enters the mind of Mark David Chapman and makes him shoot John Lennon.

Laski, on the hunt for the war criminal, teams up with Natalie Preston, who is searching for her father's killer, and Sheriff Bobby Joe Gentry, who is trying to solve multiple murders that clearly involve those with "the Ability." Soon the FBI, the CIA and a secret institution called The Island Club (more people with "the Ability") are involved. And the goals ramp up to include world domination. The end is extremely creepy.

The Strain, **by Guillermo Del Toro and Chuck Hogan.** In this vampire horror novel, you will find perhaps the most horrific vampires you will ever come across. A parasitic disease overtakes Manhattan; it turns out to be part of a plot by an ancient rogue vampire and an American corporate executive who wishes to live forever. The vampires turn in seven days and by the third day they can no longer speak; they can't abide silver or the sun. They become true demon monsters with a terrifying stinger that comes out of their mouth and bites people. They are zombie-like and no longer truly sentient. A CDC worker teams up with a rodent exterminator and a Holocaust survivor who has tracked these creatures since World War II. The three attempt to free Manhattan of the creatures. By the end of book one, many monsters are dead, but Manhattan is still under siege. There is nothing conflicted or redeeming about these monsters, no thought, and no possibility of redemption—just a black-and-white struggle against evil. The plot is gripping; I have not read the sequels.

Let the Right One In, **by John Ajvide Lindqvist.** This is a wonderful novel from Sweden that features a young-looking, voracious vampire. It's very much a horror story, in the sense that the young vampire "child" of unclear gender and age is a force of nature with no moral qualms. But the book is also a beautifully told morality tale of what happens to the bullied child. The Swedish version of the movie (there is also an American version) is exquisite, if terrifying.

Lost Souls, **by Poppy Z. Brite.** This is a true horror novel, but the writing is lyrical, dark, and smoky. It takes place in the French Quarter in New Orleans and in Missing Mile, North Carolina.

The most remarkable character is Ghost, a young sensitive, who can pick up the thoughts and feelings of both the living and dead. Then there is his partner, Steve; they have a rock band called the Lost Souls. Into this situation comes Nothing, a young man who grew up as Jason but has no idea where he is really from. Nothing turns out to be the son of a woman named Jessy who was impregnated by a vampire and died after she gave birth. These vampires are another species, and humans who are impregnated by vampires cannot survive. They are not the undead, and many of the gothic myths do not apply. In a dark, mystical, Southern horror scene we see the coming together of Christian—a three-hundred-year-old vampire who is a bartender, but who has been mostly alone—and three really evil vamps who kill wantonly, as well as the beautiful Zillah, who impregnated Jessy. All these lives come together in a horrible finale that leaves several characters dead. But there is an evocative sense of young lost souls who are wandering, desperate for love. I list this title among my favorites in "The Best" section.

Revamp, **by Beck Sherman.** This is a recent, fascinating vampire novel, overly long, but well done. The heroine is in college, and yet, like several other dystopian vampire novels, once the vampire aspects get going, she leaves her old life and we never hear from any of the characters we meet when the world was normal. After she turns in her last paper to a professor who has turned ominously strange, she boards a plane to L.A. and the horror begins. Emma, our heroine, wakes up in an empty plane and finds herself escaping from strange people, including a sadistic gynecologist. At first she doesn't believe that these people are vampires who are taking over the planet, and even after she teams up with a small group of vampire hunters, she is skeptical. But eventually she comes to terms with it. Vampires are breeding humans for blood. In a manner of weeks the whole world has changed. These vampires do not have magical or super powers and we never really learn why they have chosen this moment to take over the world. Emma is a feisty protagonist with comic flair. There are many good characters and complex relationships. Emma grows and develops as she trains to be a trusted member of the team of hunters. When one or two of the team members are turned, it is unclear whether or not there can be some good vampires. Some reviewers have compared the novel to the film *Daybreakers*.

The Accursed, by Joyce Carol Oates. This is the latest in her *Belle-fleur* saga, and I confess I haven't read the others. It's not clear if it's really a vampire novel, although demons of all kinds populate the book, and a few of them seem to have eternal life. It is a sprawling gothic horror novel that takes place in Princeton in the years 1905–6. The novel is filled with historical characters: Woodrow Wilson, when he was president of Princeton, Grover Cleveland, Mark Twain, Jack London, and the socialist and muckraker Upton Sinclair. The story is about a demonic curse that falls over Princeton. There are almost no sympathetic characters, and the amount of misogyny (appropriate to the times, of course), racism, and anti-Semitism described in the book is almost unbearable. The stifling upper-class society is so rigid that none of these matters can be openly discussed until the curse is bubbling over everywhere and can't be dismissed. Some beautiful writing, but a most odd book.

HUMOROUS NOVELS for ADULTS— LIGHT, FRIVOLOUS, and FUN

Authors:

Christopher Moore, MaryJanice Davidson, Molly Harper, Gerry Bartlett, Terry Pratchett

THESE NOVELS RANGE from lovely and humorous to silly and mediocre. Some of the best are by Christopher Moore.

***Bloodsucking Fiends: A Love Story, You Suck: A Love Story,* and *Bite Me: A Love Story,* by Christopher Moore.** They all take place in San Francisco, and the main vampires, Tommy Flood and the Countess, definitely try to do the right thing, but they are also attacked by vampires with a dark side. The best thing Moore does is resurrect the character of Emperor Norton, a real historical figure from the 19th century who claimed to be emperor of San Francisco. The city humored him (this is true!) by accepting his currency and posting his proclamations. In this saga, the emperor is sweet but crazy. He travels around with his two dogs, whom he calls "his men," and they try to rid the society of evil vampires, including (in the last book) vampire cats. The novels are told in the voice of various characters and are filled with street language, as well as Goth and teen slang.

Undead and Unwed, **by MaryJanice Davidson.** This is the first of Davidson's long series of books with "undead" in the title. *Undead and Unemployed* and *Undead and Unpopular* are among many others. They are frothy, light, with too much fashion. I didn't want to go past the first one.

The Jane Jameson series, by Molly Harper. Molly Harper has written three quirky and humorous books, *Nice Girls Don't Have Fangs, Nice Girls Don't Date Dead Men,* and *Nice Girls Don't Live Forever.* Jane Jameson is a recently fired librarian who gets drunk at a local bar in a small Southern town called the Hallows. She meets Gabriel Nightingale, then leaves the bar somewhat drunk, drives her car into a ditch, and gets mistaken for a deer and shot by some random hunter. Dying, she is rescued by Gabriel, who turns out to be a vampire. He turns her. The rest of the book is her attempt to adjust to her new situation. There's her relationship with Gabriel, her relationship with another vampire named Dick, and a series of traumatic events where she is set up and falsely accused of several vampire murders. During all this she is looking for a job and pretending she is normal to her parents. The book has flair, lots of fun literary references, and nerdy, bookish talk. And after having read many bad vampire romance novels, I found myself feeling waves of relief that our heroine hadn't had sex for three years—and no good sex at that. She does finally get it on with Gabriel. The scenes with her parents are extremely funny.

In the second book, *Nice Girls Don't Date Dead Men,* we learn vampires can't vote and can't legally marry, unless they were married before they came "out" into the world. Half of Jane's family doesn't know she is a vampire; the other half hasn't come to terms with it. Jane's mom is still sending over food, even though she knows Jane can't eat; her sister won't talk to her. Jane helps run an occult bookstore that she turns into a success. Meanwhile Gabriel, her sire and boyfriend, keeps on being mysterious and leaving on strange business trips. There are all kinds of other little oddities, and it all might be insufferable if it wasn't written with incredible wit.

In the third book we get to the bottom of Gabriel's disappearances; there are killings and abductions, and a very funny section involving a meeting of the local Chamber of Commerce that seems more like a gathering of Mary Kay cosmetics salespeople. Although these books are pure fluff, the humor works.

Real Vampires Have Curves, by Gerry Bartlett. Lightweight and without the humor or literary flair of Harper's books, *Real Vampires Have Curves,* the first of a series, features Glory St. Clair, a vampire who moves to Austin and opens a vintage clothing store called Vintage Vamp's Emporium. Turned in Shakespeare's time, she was "full-figured" when she was turned, unlike many of the thin people and vampires around her, and so she will be forever, but still she is gorgeous and blond and a size 12! (Speaking as someone who finally achieved my WeightWatchers goal after decades, but has never gone below a 14, full-figured? Give me a break!) Vampires can go to church, and don't seem to mind crosses, but they do sleep like the dead when the sun is up, and can be staked. They can move fast, are strong, and can shape-shift with practice, although Glory hasn't yet gained many of these abilities. She has to avoid vampire hunters and choose among suitors. The various sex scenes are formulaic; this is another book with sentences like "I loved the way he filled me," which seems an unfortunate staple of the vampire romance genre and makes me want to gag. Glory is reasonably funny, sassy, and determined to be independent, but I don't have any desire to read the rest of the series.

The Discworld series, by Terry Pratchett. There could not be any list of comic novels without Terry Pratchett, an English fantasy novelist best known for his Discworld series, and the second most widely read author in the UK. Several of the Discworld novels have vampire characters. *Monstrous Regiment* is an anti-war and anti-authoritarian send-up, the fantasy tale of a girl, Polly Perks, who disguises herself as a boy to join a regiment and find her brother, only to discover that most of regiment is doing the same thing. Even the male vampire turns out to be female, and quite a lovely character at that.

Carpe Jugulum is a Discworld novel full of vampires and witches. I list this title among my favorites in "The Best" section. The witches are lovely; the vampires are not. They come from Überwald and are classically gothic, unlike some other vampires Prachett writes about. Despite the "gothic" traits, they are oddly modern and have trained themselves to tolerate garlic, lemons, daylight, and some religious symbols. They can fly and are powerful. King Verence invites a family of vampires to the christening of his daughter, but they then attempt to take over the whole country.

Four witches attempt to turn the tide and they finally get the most powerful witch, Granny Weatherwax, a truly remarkable elderly woman, to save the day, along with the help of a reluctant priest. The best parts of the novel are Pratchett's insights about religion, witchcraft, and good and evil. Here is a wonderful quote from Granny Weatherwax, speaking to a priest on the subject of what it would mean if you really *knew* that your god was real:

> Now if I'd had seen him, really there, really alive it'd be in me like a fever. If I thought there was some god who really did care two hoots about people, who watched 'em like a father and really cared for 'em like a mother . . . well, you wouldn't catch me sayin' things like "there are two sides to every question" and "we must respect other people's beliefs." You wouldn't find me being gen'rally nice in the hope that it'd turn out all right in the end. Not if that flame was burning in me like an unforgivin' sword. And I did say burnin', Mr. Oats, 'cos that's what it'd be. You say that you people don't burn folk and sacrifice people anymore, but that's what true faith would mean, y'see. Sacrificin' your own life, one day at a time, to the flame, declarin' the truth of it, workin' for it, breathin' the soul of it. That's religion. Anything else is just . . . is just bein' nice. And a way of keepin' in touch with the neighbors.

You can't say it much better than that.

YOUNG ADULT FICTION

THIS CATEGORY IS SO VAST, I am putting it into many sub-categories, including Nerdy, Geeky Vampires; Vampires at School; Hogwarts for Vampires (or Vampires at Vampire School); Coming-of-Age Vampire Novels; and Young Adult Romance. Many books fall into more than one category.

Nerdy, Geeky Vampires

Authors:

Kimberly Pauley, Brian Meehl, Heather Brewer, Adam Rex, Catherine Jinks, Alan Forsyth, James Patrick Brotherton and Darren Shan

Some of the best recent vampire novels are for teens, and my favorites are novels that turn the genre on its head. These include *Sucks to Be Me* and *Still Sucks to Be Me,* by Kimberly Pauley, and *Suck It Up* by Brian Meehl.

***Sucks to Be Me* and *Still Sucks to Be Me,* by Kimberly Pauley.** Pauley imagines some dreary, all-too-normal, nerdy vampires in the regular day-to-day world. In *Sucks to Be Me,* the heroine finds out her parents are vampires and she has to make a choice: to be or not to be. It's not as easy as it seems, and the book is laugh-out-loud funny.

In the sequel, *Still Sucks to Be Me,* the heroine becomes a vampire but has to fake her death, leave her friends, live in a yucky town, and still obey her parents. I liked both books, but *Sucks to Be Me* was my favorite. I list both among my favorites in "The Best" section.

Suck It Up, by Brian Meehl. *Suck It Up* stars a pimply, unattractive, geeky vampire. If you get turned at fifteen, you keep your acne for life! He still manages to become the first officially "outed" vampire in the world.

The Chronicles of Vladimir Tod series, by Heather Brewer. In this series, there is a book for each grade from eigth grade through high school: *Eighth Grade Bites, Ninth Grade Slays, Tenth Grade Bleeds, Eleventh Grade Burns,* and *Twelfth Grade Kills.* These are rather lovely books with a half-vampire boy who still seems to have all the powers of a vampire, but can stay out in the sun with sunscreen. Vlad can float and read minds, but he doesn't seem all that strong and still gets bullied at school. Like the vampire kid in *Suck It Up,* he is not very attractive and has all the typical teen problems, trying to be liked, trying to get a girl. At the same time, he has to guard his secret from most of his friends. He drinks blood from a fridge, and his aunt, a nurse, procures it from a hospital and puts it in his ordinary food so it isn't noticed. There are fine sequences when he has to face the Slayer Society and when he gets trained by his uncle. By book four things turn darker (don't they always! Think of Harry Potter.) Vlad is on trial for killing a vampire and telling humans the truth; he is also stalked by a slayer who was once a good friend. He starts feeding on some humans and even participates in a hunt. In the last book, things come to a head in unexpected ways and nothing is what it seems.

Fat Vampire, **by Adam Rex.** As you can probably tell by the title, this book is also in the genre of nerdy anti-type vampires, and although it's not in the league of *Suck It Up* and *Sucks to Be Me,* it's a reasonably funny story about a short, not-so-attractive fifteen-year-old who is turned into a vampire. We also meet his human friend Jay and his love interest from India, a girl named Sejal. Fun moments include an appearance at the *Rocky Horror Show* and a comic convention, and there are some astute passages about Goth and geek culture. Doug, the teen vampire, changes as he feeds more; he can turn into a bat and become mist, but he also becomes less human and less agreeable as he goes through these changes. In the end he wants out.

Reformed Vampire Support Group, **by Catherine Jinks.** A fairly funny, odd book, this novel is based on a unique idea: vampires are couch potato wimps. They have given up drinking human blood and drink only the blood of guinea pigs, which they breed. They are weak and sickly, get dizzy and nauseous, take lots of special enzymes, and have to live very closeted lives. These vampires are dead during the day. At night they don't do much; they watch TV and go to meetings, a support group like AA, with a counselor who is a sympathetic priest. If you drink human blood, you get strong, but you endanger all other vamps. Our protagonist, Nina Harrison, looks fifteen—the age she was turned—and people treat her as a kid, although she is about fifty. She lives at home with her mortal seventy-year-old protective mother and writes vampire fantasies, which have a strong, adventurous vampire heroine named Zadia Bloodstone. When a vampire hunter comes on the scene, Nina and the support group begin taking uncharacteristic action. The idea is great; the writing is fair.

The Loneliest Vampire in NYC, by Alan Forsyth. A silly book; it would have been fine at 200 pages, but at 504 it was tedious beyond belief. It's clearly self-published and has too many typos. Our hero, Stanley, is a vampire, but all he really wants is to get a girl and he always says the wrong thing. He has a friend, Vincent, and a talking cat named Poe. He meets Anika, a reporter, but she doesn't reciprocate his feelings. Anika has heard rumors of a supernatural underground in New York City. They end up on a crazy adventure trying to defeat Doyle, an evil vampire, his partner Sylvna, and an evil creature named Nyx. They end up in parallel worlds with different versions of the evil characters, and even different versions of themselves. It's a great idea and there's even a touch of wit, but it's tiresome by the end.

Reclaiming the Dead, by James Patrick Brotherton. This is an extremely odd vampire book. We start with Merton Daniels, a nerdy kid who doesn't function well, and his roommate, Coaler. Merton is one of these guys who can't strike up a conversation with a girl, has snot running from his nose, and does everything wrong. The first part of the book is really fun; the conversations between Coaler and Merton remind one of *The Big Bang Theory.* After Merton is fired from his job, and totally down and out, he meets someone who offers him a job: reclaiming the dead. He is told he will be notified of his assignments. He gets addresses to go to where he finds vampires asleep; he can kill them and pillage all their possessions. He is totally freaked at first, and he and Coaler botch a few attempts, but he begins to get it down and learns his trade. He generally sets fires. He refuses to stake the vampires. The second part of the book gets weirder. We meet a creature from the ancient world, perhaps Judas. He has been turned into a very strong vampire who can morph into all kinds of creatures. We watch him kill and go on a rampage. In part three, we return to Merton, who tries to confront and kill this ancient, terrifying creature. Merton matures and strikes up a conversation with a girl. He find peace and becomes whole. We never know if he continues his job as a slayer.

The Saga of Darren Shan: Cirque du Freak series, by Darren Shan. This series includes a dozen adventure novels; I read the first three: *A Living Nightmare, The Vampire's Assistant,* and *Tunnels of Blood.* They feature a boy who, against his will, gets turned into a half vampire and becomes a vampire's assistant to save the life of his somewhat disreputable and perhaps evil friend. The first book begins at a freak show, when Darren's best friend recognizes one of the entertainers as a vampire from a 19th-century painting. This friend wants to become a vampire, but the vampire in question refuses to turn him. They steal the vampire's poisonous performing spider. The spider bites his friend, who is quickly paralyzed and is dying. That is what leads Darren to accept a deal with the vampire, fake his own death, and become the vampire's assistant. As a half vampire, Darren has strength, and he can still go out into the sun. But it is a lonely life.

In the second volume, *The Vampire's Assistant*, Darren Shan travels with his vampire companion, Mr. Crepsley. He reunites with the Cirque du Freak and befriends the snake boy and two human friends, Sam and RV. His big struggle is over drinking human blood, which he believes will turn him evil, but he knows it is something he must eventually do or else die. He believes that just thinking of humans as food will remove him from humanity. This is a far more interesting book than the first novel, because it involves Darren's struggle to find friendship and the disastrous paths he takes in the end. The Cirque, which seemed just a horror show in the first book, has complex beings, many surprisingly moral.

In book three, *Tunnels of Blood*, Mr. Crepsley is out every night on some mysterious mission. When six bodies are found by the police, drained of blood, Darren is convinced that Crepsley is the murderer, but there is another evil out there, and things are more complex than they seem. The books are short, easy to read, but not very well written.

Vampires at School

Authors:

Stephenie Meyer (*see* Coming-of-Age), Rachel Caine, L. J. Smith, Melissa de la Cruz, Alyson Noël, Amelia Atwater-Rhodes, RaShelle Workman (*see* Supernatural Fantasy)

These are all novels that, like the TV series *Buffy the Vampire Slayer* and *The Vampire Diaries*, take place in a normal school setting. The Twilight Saga is also in this genre. This sets them apart from another series of teen vampire novels that I dub "Hogwarts for Vampires, or

Vampires at Vampire School." I will talk about the Twilight Saga in the Coming-of-Age Vampire Novels section, but much of it takes place at the local high school in Forks, Washington.

The Morganville Vampire series, by Rachel Caine. The heroine is Claire Danvers, a student at Texas Prairie University, who finds that her town, Morganville, Texas, is controlled by vampires. I found the first book, *Glass Houses,* very difficult because Danvers experiences extreme bullying by mean girls that ends in physical violence. This might seem believable in middle school, and in high school, but, except for fraternity hazing, is bullying prevalent in college? I know no one who has experienced it. Danvers leaves her dorm of horrors and moves into a house with three odd roommates. The books apparently get more interesting and complex as they go on. I didn't.

The Vampire Diaries, by L. J. Smith. This young adult series started with four short novels, *The Awakening, The Struggle, The Fury,* and *Dark Reunion.* The story involves a town that has had a history of vampire families as well as witches and werewolves. There is a lovely protagonist, Elena, and the vampire Salvatore brothers, Stefan and Damon. There is a television show based on the books. In many ways the TV show, which is popular internationally, is better than the books. In the show, Elena comes off as a serious and intense person and Damon and Stefan are total eye candy. When the show begins, one of them is good and one of them is evil, but both become much more complex as the seasons go on.

The Blue Bloods series, by Melissa de la Cruz. Perhaps the oddest series of books featuring vampires at school is Blue Bloods by Melissa de la Cruz. Imagine *Gossip Girl* plus vampires. The series is based on an idea so completely outrageous, it almost works. It turns out that the families that came over on the *Mayflower* are really vampires, reincarnating over and over. So, many of the people going to elite private schools on the Upper East Side of Manhattan, and carrying those Prada bags, are really—you guessed it—vampires. (Perhaps that's why they don't eat much and look like social X-rays!) But besides being the reincarnation of Pilgrims like Myles Standish, the author presupposes that these vampires go back so far that they are the reincarnation of the original archangels. East Side socialites as vampires? That's totally believable. Archangels? No way! I read the first four books in this series: *Bluebloods, Masquerade, Revelations,* and *The Van Alen Legacy.*

The Immortals series, by Alyson Noël. This young adult series is not particularly good, though the books are best-sellers. In the first book, *Evermore,* Ever is a teenager in high school. She seems to be a mix of Sookie Stackhouse and Bella Swan. After her parents and sister died in a car crash, she moves to California to live with an aunt. She has blamed herself for her parents' death ever since the crash. She can read people's minds and can see her dead sister, Riley. She hides under a hoodie and is considered a freak at school. At school she comes across a six-hundred-year-old immortal named Damen who is incredibly beautiful, and there is a long saga of their on-again, off-again relationship. He is not a vampire and doesn't suck blood, but he does drink a red sparkly liquid.

There is another immortal named Drina, who is out to kill Ever because she has gotten in the way of Drina's many-lifetimes-long desire for Damen. It's pretty sappy and some reviewers have called it a *Twilight* rip-off, but it's also a *True Blood* rip-off. There's lots of stuff on chakras and reincarnation, and Damen is always pulling tulips out of everything like a magician. He also keeps on disappearing, giving no reason for most of his actions. It's pretty weak.

The Den of Shadows Quartet, by Amelia Atwater-Rhodes. This series is, as you might suspect from the title, four novels. The first novel, written when she was just thirteen, has nothing to do with school. *In the Forests of the Night* is a very short novel, 146 pages, featuring Risika, a three-hundred-year-old vampire who lives in Concord, Massachusetts. Her only friend is a tiger named Tora at the zoo in New York City. Risika can change into animal form and enter the minds of people and vampires; she looks hazy in mirrors, sleeps during the day, but can be out in the sun a bit. She doesn't like garlic because her senses are so acute, but none of the other Christian and gothic aspects (holy water, churches, crosses, stakes, etc.) seem to apply. The book is the story of her transformation three hundred years ago, and her nemesis, another vampire named Aubrey. The writing is uneven, as might be expected of a thirteen-year-old author, but has potential.

Demon in My View, the second book in the series, is about Jessica, a high school student who writes vampire novels under a pseudonym. She suddenly finds that the characters she is writing about are real, are aware of her, and might try to kill her. She discovers the vampire town that she writes about and in the end makes a choice. I found the writing uneven, but I was captivated by the characters.

In the third book, *Shattered Mirror,* Sarah Vida is a witch from a long line of vampire hunters. She meets Christopher Ravena and his sister Nissa at school and immediately realizes they are vampires, but weaker, because they do not kill and seem to drink only animal blood. Christopher falls in love with Sarah and sends her poems. Her family forbids her to have anything to do with vampires, and she sets out to hunt down a vampire, Nikolas, who turns out to be Christopher's brother. This book is really about learning that your stereotypes are untrue. All the vampires turn out to be complex; there are evil and good ones among them. But Sarah's dealing with vampires brings on the wrath of her mother, Dominique Vida, who binds Sarah's magic and wants to bring her to trial for breaking the Vida laws. This may be the best of the four.

The last book, *Midnight Predator,* is less successful. The protagonist, Turquoise Draka, is a human vampire hunter who returns to Midnight, a place where vampires keep slaves. Her goal is to kill the female vampire who used to run the place with extreme brutality. Part of the story is her attempt to get revenge; another part is her meeting with Jaguar, who now runs Midnight with a softer touch. He is a shape-shifter as well as a vampire, and he has some heart and morals, which confuses her. It's a story of her attempt to find which world she belongs to, the hunter world, the vampire world, or the human world. But she and Jaguar are the only characters that are drawn deeply, and only the middle sections at Midnight sing at all. Atwater-Rhodes, now in her twenties, is finding her voice as a writer. She does have a knack of creating some characters you care about.

Hogwarts for Vampires, or Vampires at Vampire School

Authors:

P. C. Cast and Kristin Cast, Richelle Mead, Claudia Gray

Yes, Harry Potter had his wizard school, but there are at least three series of young adult books that give vampire teens their own school.

The House of Night series, by P. C. Cast and Kristin Cast. P. C. and Kristin Cast are a mother and daughter team from Tulsa, Oklahoma. *Marked, Betrayed, Chosen, Untamed, Hunted, Tempted,* and *Burned* are the ones I've read, and there are more. Vampires are chosen almost randomly; a mark suddenly appears on their forehead, and they have to leave their schools and families and enter special academies, where they are educated and slowly change, either successfully or die. This series has lots of goddess theology and lovely ceremonies. There are different kinds of vampires, some who can be in the sun and some who can't. There are serious characters that make changes in their lives, grow, and deal with issues of morality, love, and honor. Some of these characters are human, some are monsters, and some are vampires. Among the great characters are Stevie Rae, Aphrodite, Zoey Redbird, Stark, and Rephaim. Publicly, the authors will not say if they have been involved in Wicca, or goddess spirituality, but, speaking as a practitioner, the rituals feel authentic and certainly read as if the authors have experience.

The Vampire Academy series, by Richelle Mead. This series also focuses on a vampire school. I have read the first four books: *Vampire Academy, Frostbite, Shadow Kiss,* and *Blood Promise.* The academy feels very Russian and the main protagonist is not a vampire but a particular type of human-vampire mix, a dhampir, who becomes a bodyguard for one strand of rather weak royal vampires. There are both good and evil vampires in these books.

Evernight, **by Claudia Gray.** In Gray's novel, Evernight is a school for vampires to help them adjust to the modern world. Many may look young, but they are old enough to not deal easily with technology and modern society. Suddenly, the school is taking human kids who have no idea that the majority of the students are vampires, many quite old. The book starts well, because you don't realize, at first, who is human and who is a vampire. In fact, the protagonist, Bianca, and her boyfriend, Lucas, are both not what you think. The school is filled with catty and treacherous vampires, plus a headmistress with her own agenda. There are also wraiths (ghosts) who seem to be haunting many of the human students, as well as Bianca.

By the third book, *Hourglass,* Bianca and Lucas find refuge with the Black Cross, an ancient order of vampire hunters. At first, no one realizes what Bianca is, even though she has to steal blood to survive. Both are discovered; both must flee and each goes through unexpected changes. There is some of the feeling of the Twilight Saga here, a bit of the House of Night series, and, given the notion of vampire and vampire hunter falling in love, a bit of *Romeo and Juliet* as well.

Coming-of-Age Vampire Novels

Authors:

Susan Hubbard, Julie Kagawa, Robin McKinley, David Sosnowski, Stephenie Meyer, Matt Haig, Annette Curtis Klause, Vivian Vande Velde, Gypsey Teague, Wynne Channing, Neil Gaiman

These novels all feature progatonists who grow, change, and mature as they navigate a complex world filled with vampires and humans.

***The Society of S, The Year of Disappearances,* and *The Season of Risks,* by Susan Hubbard.** All fairly literary works, by a professor of English, these are serious novels, and perhaps don't even belong in the young adult category, but they do involve the coming of age of a young adolescent in a family of vampires. The books are elusive, complex, poetic, and sophisticated. In *The Society of S*, Ariella searches for her mother and discovers that she is a half vampire. She is homeschooled by her father and slowly learns that there is an alternative society of vampires of several different types. Her father is a Sanguinist. They take supplements and tonics and don't prey on humans. But there are also Colonists and Nebulists with other values. The vampires in this world can go out in the sun with sunscreen. Their image is blurry in mirrors; they can make themselves invisible and read the thoughts of others.

In *The Year of Disappearances*, Ariella goes to live with her mother in Florida. She ends up going to college and tries to fit in. She finds that her fellow students are taking a drug that turns them into zombies.

In *The Season of Risks*, the oddest book of the three, Ari has fallen in love with an independent presidential candidate who turns out to be another vampire. They date; they go sailing. She goes to an independent, progressive college and meets Sloan, an Irish scholarship student who is also some kind of Other. Ari decides that she looks too young and wants a treatment that will change her age to twenty-two. By the end, she is part of a plot to discredit the candidate and finds herself the victim of identity theft and loss of memory.

The Blood of Eden series, by Julie Kagawa. *The Immortal Rules* and *The Eternity Cure* are the first two books in this series by Julie Kagawa, known for her Iron Fey books. I am putting this series near the top of this section, because the books are excellent. The novels could easily fit into several other categories including Supernatural Fantasy or Vampire Hunters Since Buffy. We have a heroine who starts out human and ends up vampire, who is easily as deep and rich a character as Katniss Everdeen in *The Hunger Games*. In a broken-down, dystopian world, where cities are ruled by vampires and most humans are registered (branded) and supply monthly blood, Allison Sekemoto is "unregistered" and scavenges with a small group of humans on the Fringe, outside the vampires' inner city. Food is scarce and stealing invites immediate execution. There are diseased dead creatures called rabids that, like zombies, prey on humans and to a lesser extent on vampires. Allie is attacked by a rabid and left to die, but a mysterious vampire comes to her rescue. She is forced to become what she hates. She hides what she is and joins a group of pilgrims trying to find a promised land called Eden. One of the pilgrims is Zeke, who begins falling for her. Allie is complex and cynical but can give love. The book asks the question, Now that you are a monster, what kind of a monster will you be? Can you control your hunger? Allie is a good example of the vampire who is desperately struggling to be moral despite being a predator. The relationships—both vampire and human—are complex. The dystopian world is well realized.

In the sequel, *The Eternity Cure,* Allie leaves Eden after rescuing some of the pilgrims; she is thrown out when they discover the truth of what she is. She is on the hunt for Sarren, a psychopathic vampire who has captured Kanin, the mysterious vampire who turned her. Zeke leaves Eden to find Allie, and together, along with Kanin and Allie's badass vampire brother, Jackal, they attempt to find the cure to the disease that has created the rabids. It's totally gripping with surprise twists and turns and an end that leaves you gasping. Well written with beautiful relationships, this second book explores whether Allie can master her hunger and have a deep relationship with a human being. I list this series among my favorites in "The Best" section.

The Twilight Saga, by Stephenie Meyer. The four books, *Twilight, New Moon, Eclipse,* and *Breaking Dawn,* have sold more than one hundred million copies. They are not great literature, but I confess I enjoyed them all, and picking one up at the airport in May 2009 started this whole crazy journey of mine. Not everyone likes these "sparkling vampires," but they definitely fit into my reluctant, struggling-to-be-moral vampire thesis. Elsewhere, I talk about a class analysis of the Twilight Saga and some of the spiritual implications of the books. The Cullen family is lovely, including the doctor, his wife, the handsome Edward, three other kids, and, my personal favorite,

Edward's sister, Alice Cullen. Then there are the werewolves. The werewolves and the vampires are like the Capulets and the Montagues, except in this saga, there are several outside enemies that force the two sides to come together and fight as a team. This is really a story of identity and choice, even more than a romance, which is why these books fit into three or four categories: Coming-of-Age Vampire Novels, Vampires at School, Supernatural Fantasy, and Young Adult Romance. But for me, this is the story of a nerdy outsider, a lonely only child who wants an identity larger than her boring family and school situation, and who decides that an inhuman family is more interesting than the humans around her. By becoming a vampire she transforms herself into a superhero, or goddess, the queen on the chessboard. And as a vampire she is strong, successful, and the equal of Edward. "You think this is about you, Edward," she says at the end of the third film. "It's about me and my choices." That pretty much sums up what the Twilight Saga is really about, much more so than all the arguments I've read by feminists that these books stress sexual abstinence and that Edward is a stalker. Meyer has also written a version of the first novel from Edward's point of view called *Midnight Sun.* The book got out on the Internet before it was edited, and it shows.

Sunshine, **by Robin McKinley.** A novel with many lovely qualities, it could easily fit in the Supernatural Fantasy section. The writing is quite beautiful; the main character is Sunshine, Rae Seddon, a woman who works in a bakery, whose mother is normal, but whose father is a famed magic worker. This is an alternate world that is very much like our own but has vampires who are powerful and evil. There are also all kinds of Others: demons, various sprites, and other beings. This is a world protected by wards, a kind of spell that is in objects and even tattoos. Sunshine gets captured by a vampire gang near a lake. She is imprisoned along with another vampire who becomes a strange ally. She helps him escape and, as long as he touches her, he can be in the sun. The heart of the novel is her double life, fighting this evil vampire gang secretly along with her vampire ally, Constantine, and, at the same time, being part of a very normal, coffee-shop, bread-baking world. She slowly comes to terms with her own magical powers. Constantine is scary and unattractive, with grey skin, and yet the bond between them grows strong. The main flaw in this novel is that the scenes of daily life in the bakery go on forever. But the relationship between Sunshine and Constantine, and the relationship she has with other magical workers, is beautifully drawn. The exploration of darkness and light is powerful.

Vamped, by David Sosnowski. One of the most original and completely surprising vampire novels I have read, the book takes place in a world where there are almost no humans left; vampires rule the world. There are no toilets in houses, no food, except pet food, for mortal pets, although you can still get certain things like chocolate and all kinds of stuff from the past on eBay. Vampires are strong and fast and can be killed by sunlight, beheading, and a stab to the heart. They are pale, their eyes are black, and they heal quickly. They are not affected by Christian symbols or holy water or garlic, and there are actually vampire priests and even Catholic services, although communion has clearly changed. But life is very boring for many; forever is a long time. There are also "screamers"—kids who were turned very young and are doomed to look like children forever, so they are bratty and curse a lot.

Martin Kowalski, who became a vampire during WWII and was one of those secretly responsible for giving vampires so much power, comes across a six-year-old mortal girl hiding in a hole—perhaps one of the only mortals still around. There are secret farms where very rich vampires get to buy such children, but most vampires now live on bottled blood and artificial plasma. So Marty finds this girl and, at first, thinks he will drink from her, a rare treat in this bureaucratized vamp world. But he slowly gets won over and secretly keeps her until she grows up. He has to protect her from the world that would kill her immediately if she was discovered. There are wonderful ways they get around the society; she can go out alone in the daytime and forage because all the vamps are asleep; they go to Alaska for a vacation, because it is so cold that even vampires can see their breath and she won't be discovered. This is the story of her coming of age, her first period, her first sexual encounter, her Internet friendships, and Marty's attempt to find her a mother who can be part of her world. But she's savvy and finds a lot of things out by herself. There's lots of humor. The writing is perky and smart.

***The Short Second Life of Bree Tanner,* by Stephenie Meyer.** This 178-page novella tells the story of one of the most interesting characters never really developed in the Twilight Saga. Bree is made a newborn vampire by Riley, whom Victoria turns to create an army to take down the Cullens, and most particularly Bella. We see the newborn army from the inside, very terrifying and out of control, constantly in chaos, setting fires and killing each other. Riley keeps the newborns ignorant—for example, they don't know they can go out into the sun. They can't remember much about their old life, and the thirst for blood controls them. They constantly violate the main vampire rule—to be discreet—and they create carnage wherever they go. During the war with the Cullens, Bree surrenders but must face the ultimate punishment of the Volturi. This book is better written than much of the Twilight Saga, or perhaps Bree is simply a very compelling character, a bundle of fear and innocence, way over her head.

The Radleys, by Matt Haig. A recent novel by an English author, it was seriously reviewed in *The New York Times.* It takes place over one week in a small suburban English village. It concerns a family of vampires who are "abstainers"; they do not drink blood and have not told their two children the true facts of their existence. Because they abstain, they shorten their lives, and the kids are sickly and have rashes. These vampires are allergic to garlic; they have to wear serious sunblock and stay out of the sun, although they have no problems with crosses or holy water. They can also obtain vampire blood, exchanging it with others and drinking it from bottles once a week. The daughter, Clara, not knowing her real needs, becomes a vegan on principle, making herself even more ill. The children are considered freaks at school; animals fear them and birds do not sing around them. At one point, when Clara is attacked and is about to be raped, she suddenly bites her attacker, drains and kills him; she is suddenly transformed, strengthened, and is in shock, not knowing what has happened. Her parents finally tell her the truth and call on outside help from a relative, as a police investigation begins.

One clear theme is how the Radleys find a way to live in both worlds. The ending is lovely and somewhat unexpected.

***The Silver Kiss,* by Annette Curtis Klause.** Klause has written four books; this lovely young adult novel is her only vampire novel, published in 1990. Klause has said that her own fantasies go toward werewolves. She has a werewolf book, *Blood and Chocolate,* which has been well received. I have described the plot in the opening essay. To summarize briefly, Zoe is a teen whose mother is dying of cancer. Her father is remote and her best friend is moving away. No one will talk about death. Zoe meets Simon, a very lonely vampire who has constantly been on the move and has been hunting for his villainous brother. His brother was turned as a six-year-old and has been on a killing spree; he's killed many women, including their own mother. Zoe and Simon slowly bond; he tells her some of his three-hundred-year history. They talk about death and she comes to terms with the death of her mother. Zoe and Simon can share their loneliness and they can speak about death. Their relationship allows Zoe to come into her own, to have the talks that need to take place with her mother and father, and to confront the truth of her situation.

***Companions of the Night,* by Vivian Vande Velde.** Though this novel is not really a coming-of-age story, it does involve a teen facing moral choices and it's lovely. Kerry Nowicki is sixteen. One night, although she has only a learner's permit, she takes the family car to fetch her little brother's stuffed animal that he left in the laundry. Suddenly, the owner of the laundry and several other men drag a man in his twenties into the laundry; they claim he is a vampire and they are going to kill him by leaving him out in the sun. They are convinced Kerry is a vampire, too. Ethan, the guy, is wounded and seems totally normal, so she helps free him, but soon she doesn't trust him, and she returns home a day later to find that her dad and brother have been kidnapped. On her mirror are scrawled the words: "Vampire, we have your family." She soon discovers Ethan *is* a vampire; there is little trust between them. The relationship is complex but she promises to help him if he will help find her family. There are large issues of morality, killing, lying, and trust. The story is also about the choices one must make that are not dictated by history or family. The tension between Kerry and Ethan is never really resolved.

Fangs & Claws, **by Gypsey Teague.** This self-published digital novel is really two stories, but both work. Teague, the author, is known in the occult world for creating a system of magic called "Steampunk Magic." The book starts in Nazi Germany, with the creation by the SS of a vampire race of soldiers. The book quickly turns to the present, where Jennifer Chamberlain, a college student, is writing an essay for a professor who comes from Germany, in which she argues that the greatest impact for good of WWII was the creation by the Nazis of a nonliving but not-quite-undead vampire race. She convinces her professor to turn her, not an easy quest—she asks many times, but there are legal contracts involved and permissions to get. Her parents practically disown her when they find out. The first half of the book is the story of her parents' quest to turn her back to human. They are finally convinced they cannot stop her. Chamberlain goes to work for a famous vampire publishing house in Seattle and ends up researching old journals that lead her to seek the first, or near first vampire, a quest that leads her to Eastern Europe. But the clues are much closer than you might think. The book falls into the category of "woman scholar" vampire books, like *A Discovery of Witches* by Deborah Harkness and *The Historian* by Elizabeth Kostova. It works well.

***What Kills Me,* by Wynne Channing.** This is well written and I admit I slurped it up in a long afternoon. Our protagonist, Axelia, or Zee for short, is in Rome studying Italian. Thinking she might want to do something a little risky, she sneaks out for an evening meeting with an Italian young man, Paolo, who turns out not only to be a vampire, but also one whose job, we later learn, involves procuring food for others, and he attempts to kill her. He brings her to an old church where she tries to escape but falls into a deep well of blood and is mysteriously turned. The vampires in this world have a rigid hierarchy, a ruling Empress, and a general, and every vampire must have a sire, or at least a guardian. By falling into a sacred well of blood of ancient vampires, and becoming a vampire alone, Zee is a renegade. And there's a prophecy saying that a renegade vampire will kill the entire vampire race. So the vampire hierarchy is out to kill her. The book is filled with battles; Zee eventually learns to fight and become stronger. She also finds out that she has special powers, including the ability to be in the sun. There is a definite resonance with some of the ideas about ancient vampires in Anne Rice's work.

The Graveyard Book, by Neil Gaiman. This is the story of a little child whose parents are brutally murdered; you never learn completely why. He escapes into a graveyard and, after much debate, is adopted by all the dead residents. He is named Nobody Owens, or Bod for short. His guardian is a wonderful vampire named Silas. Although the word "vampire" is never used in the book, we know that Silas has no reflection, has pale skin like ivory, is cold to the touch, wears black velvet, and can travel the worlds of the living and the dead. He tells Bod that he was once monstrous, but in this book he serves a totally moral role. Bod can speak with the dead and he learns many skills, like how to fade and become invisible. He is still being sought by the murderers, a secret order, and Bod is protected only while in the graveyard. He tries to go to school and has many adventures. As he grows up the dead start disappearing to him; eventually he is forced to leave the graveyard and make his way into the world.

Young Adult Romance

Authors:

Amanda Hocking, Stephenie Meyer (*see* Coming-of-Age Vampire Novels), L. J. Smith (*see* Vampires at School)

The My Blood Approves series, by Amanda Hocking. I have put most of the teen romance in other sections such as Coming-of-Age Vampire Novels, and Vampires at School. But here's a series that doesn't quite fit in those other categories. Amanda Hocking has written a bunch of novels, many self-published: *My Blood Approves,*

Fate, Flutter, Wisdom, and *Letters to Elise: a Peter Townsend Novella.*
Hocking self-published *My Blood Approves,* and soon she had made
$2 million. Now St. Martin's is publishing her paranormal fiction.
My Blood Approves, the first of the series, has some elements of *Twilight:* a girl in high school, and more than one gorgeous vampire.
It has a bit of the Argeneau Vampire series (see Adult Romance),
since you meet your soul mate, although in this series it is the
blood that calls to blood. The vampires can be in the sun, although
it tires them. They are strong, heal fast, and find immortality as
much of a curse as a blessing. Mae, Ezra, Peter, and Jack are a vampire family, not by blood. They are rich, and humans are drawn
to them. Unlike the Cullens, they drink human blood, although
the younger ones use vampire blood banks, and the older ones go
to clubs where there are willing donors. They don't kill and need
blood only once a week. Alice Bonhom meets Jack, who saves her
life, and while she finds him attractive, and comes to love him, she
becomes totally obsessed with his "brother" Peter. Mae and Ezra
love her like a daughter and want her to be part of their family.
She eventually finds out that they are vampires, and she is asked to
make a decision. There are lots of typos and the book could use a
good editor, but it's quite an angst-filled teenage page-turner.

In *Fate,* Alice's gay brother is in a serious accident and ends up
being turned before her. He becomes part of the vampire family
and becomes a more mature and more interesting person. Alice is
depressed and alienated; her blood moves toward Peter, her heart
toward Jack. At the end the choice is made suddenly, and Alice's
world changes in the way you just knew it would. Again, there are
a ridiculous number of grammatical errors and simple typos.

Flutter is the best of the lot, because it actually deals with complex relationships. Peter leaves on a suicide mission and takes on some rapacious vampires called lycans. He is rescued by Alice and Ezra. Milo, Alice's gay brother, who was turned first, has a human boyfriend who almost dies when Milo drinks too much from him. Alice also has trouble mastering bloodlust. The entire family breaks up over a decision to turn a five-year-old terminally ill relative.

In *Wisdom,* the five-year-old child who is turned creates havoc; there is an encounter with vampire vigilantes—essentially bounty hunters—and Alice and Milo find out they, themselves, are not quite what they think they are.

Letters to Elise: A Peter Townsend Novella is a small book, again self-published, with lots of typos and grammatical errors, but clearly written to deal with what we might call the Team Peter phenomenon. Just as there is Team Jacob and Team Edward in the Twilight Saga, people reading Hocking have bonded with either Jack or Peter. This is a book totally based on letters to Elise, the vampire Peter fell in love with in the 19th century, and who died eleven years later. It's a way of telling Peter's perspective on events in previous books. The novella fills in some gaps, but *Letters to Elise* is not a very good book.

ADULT ROMANCE

Authors:

Nora Roberts, Karen Essex, Lynsay Sands, Deborah Harkness, Morna McDermott, Meg Cabot, Jeaniene Frost (*see* Detective Vampire Fiction), Christine Feehan, J. R. Ward, Kresley Cole, Lara Adrian

VAMPIRE ROMANCE novels are ubiquitous; they range from the lovely and poetic to books so awful you want to throw them in the trash after only a few pages. Some of them verge on porn, with each one having two or three, occasionally even a dozen, totally predictable sex scenes. But there are also wonderful novels that fall into the Adult Romance category.

I put my favorites first. Also, I put some novels that could be considered romance in other sections. The Vampire Empire series by the Griffiths is science fiction and alternate history as well as romance. The Southern Vampire Mysteries series by Charlaine Harris goes with regional novels, along with the Chicagoland Vampires series and the Vampires of New England series, although romance plays an important part in all of them.

The Circle Trilogy, by Nora Roberts. This series includes *Morrigan's Cross, Dance of the Gods,* and *Valley of Silence.* I loved these books; I list this series among my favorites in "The Best" section. I confess, I had never read a Nora Roberts novel. What can you say about an author who has written more than two hundred books in less than thirty years? At first, I assumed she had a stable of writers and I was tempted to be snide, but I was so intrigued that I looked her up to discover she writes eight hours a day, even when on vacation. In the end, I was totally swept up by the story, the relationships, the characters, and the writing. We start in 12th-century Ireland where Hoyt Mac Cionaoith, a sorcerer, is angry and filled with guilt that he did not save his brother, Cian, from being turned into a vampire by the evil vampire Lilith. The goddess Morrigan sends Hoyt on a quest to save the world from Lilith's vampire army. He has to step through time into our modern world and form a circle of six warriors—a witch, a demon hunter, a shapeshifter, etc. He ends up in contemporary New York where he meets both his vampire brother who has lived one thousand years and who, surprisingly, joins the battle against Lilith, and Glenna, a witch with whom Hoyt subsequently falls in love. Two members of the team come from a fabled fantasy land called Geall, including the queen of her people, Moira, and her shapeshifter brother, Larkin. The last member is Blair, a modern demon hunter who comes from the Midwest. The relationship between Hoyt and Glenna is beautiful, and their handfasting at the end of the first book seemed so right, it reminded me of some ceremonies I had experienced in the contemporary Pagan movement. And Geall is clearly a Pagan land. Cian, the vampire, is a solitary and lonely character through his one thousand years. The descriptions of life, nature, the different times, and different worlds are enthralling.

Book two is even better. If *Morrigan's Cross* concentrated on the relationship between the sorcerer Hoyt and the modern witch, Glenna, the second book concentrates on Blair, the demon hunter, and Larkin, the shapeshifter from Geall. Unlike the Jeaniene Frost series, described elsewhere, Nora Roberts mutes the sex and violence. While there is fighting aplenty, she instead concentrates on relationships filled with compassion and complexity. In this second book, Blair heals the hurts that came from her father's abandonment and comes to know true love for the first time.

The third book may be the best of the lot, emphasizing the relationship between Moira, the queen of Geall, and the vampire, Cian, the brother of Hoyt, the loneliest of the six. All this takes place while they forge a battle plan to save all three worlds—modern and ancient Ireland, Geall, and contemporary New York—as they fight the vampire Lilith and her army. There are passages in this book that are truly inspired and that are unlike any other descriptions I have read of love between human and vampire, including an extraordinary scene where Cian shows Moira the beauty of her own body, by loving her in a mirror where only she is reflected. Although battles are waged and people die, there is a sense of hope, compassion, beauty, and love that overrides all.

Dracula in Love, **by Karen Essex.** My second favorite in the romance genre is a feminist tour de force. Beautifully written, it turns the entire Dracula saga on its head and is at once sensual, erotic, and feminist. Without giving away too much of the plot, this is a story where Dracula gets his power and immortality from a woman; there are chilling scenes, but the real horror turns out to be not Dracula, but Dr. Seward and Von Helsinger, who represent a medical profession that tries to cure women of their sexual desires (hysteria) through methods that can only be described as physical and mental torture. The scenes in the asylum were so scary that I almost couldn't turn the pages; the scenes with the count were incredibly gentle in comparison. Mina is a complex figure who grows throughout the book; Harker is simply a tool. The writing has a Victorian sensibility and is very lyrical, and the language and descriptions feel historically accurate in tone. This is a very satisfying novel. I list this title among my favorites in "The Best" section.

A Discovery of Witches, by Deborah Harkness. This book has romance, but so much more. This is the first book in the All Souls Trilogy, written by a historian of science at USC. It has been described as *Twilight* for intellectuals, and there is a tiny bit of truth to that assessment. But the writing is much better and it seamlessly weaves together history, hard science, scholarship, alchemy, and a magical world of witches, vampires, and daemons. I list this title among my favorites in "The Best" section. The main protagonist is Diana Bishop, a historian from an old witch family dating back to Salem. She has rejected her supernatural ancestry (her parents were murdered during a magical spell in Africa), and she has avoided using or even learning about her own powers. Instead, she has immersed herself in academia, studying in Oxford, England, at the Bodleian Library. When she orders up a book, Ashmole 782, she realizes it is magically charged and has missing pages. The book has been lost for centuries, and unbeknownst to her, she is the first to be able to call it up. Her action stirs up the supernatural world, and, suddenly, witches, vampires, and daemons are all over the library. She meets a very handsome Oxford geneticist, a vampire named Matthew, and they begin a very complex and torrid relationship over the next forty days while various witches and vampires hunt them down, partly because they want the book, believing it carries the secret of their origins, and partly because the relationship between Matthew and Diana violates an ancient covenant. This is the beginning of a sprawling adventure that combines the supernatural with discussions of Darwin, genetics, fine wines (Harkness writes a wine blog), and more. Diana reluctantly and fearfully begins to access her own witchy powers. The first book has wonderful scenes—a hilarious description of a yoga class for supernaturals, for example. The characters that compose Diana's witch family in New York and Matthew's complex vampire family in France are interesting enough to make you care. The end is a cliff-hanger and the couple flees into the past. By the way, there really was an Ashmole 782, and it really is missing.

Shadow of Night, the second book in the All Souls Trilogy, starts where *A Discovery of Witches* left off; the couple lands in Matthew's house in Woodstock, England, in the year 1590. We learn that Matthew has been a warrior, knight, spy, prince, and member of the shadowy Congregation that enforces the rules of the supernatural world. We are among a huge assortment of historical figures: Queen Elizabeth, Christopher Marlowe, and Sir Walter Raleigh, just to mention a few. Matthew and Diana spend time in England, France, and the court of the Holy Roman Empire in

Prague—all in a quest to find Ashmole 782 and witches that can help Diana control her growing and unruly abilities. Matthew is a Catholic in Protestant England; Diana is a witch at the same time that witches are being executed in Scotland and brought up for questioning even in London. Both are on dangerous ground that is constantly shifting. Matthew in the 16th century is not as liberated as he was in the 21st, and their marriage has rocky moments. In addition, they are confronted emotionally by meeting important relatives from their past that are dead in the modern world, and they must be careful not to interfere so much that the past will be changed. When the couple finally comes across Ashmole 782, it is for too short a time to penetrate its secrets, but the few things Matthew and Diana learn are deeply disturbing and unexpected.

At nearly six hundred pages, the book is so complex that there is a list of eighty-five characters at the end—thirty-seven are historical figures—too many. You had only about a dozen characters to care about in the first book. But anyone with a huge interest in Shakespearean England will find a host of fascinating details and descriptions.

The Sacrament, **by Morna McDermott.** This book was self-published and the story is quite original. Campbell is a woman academic living with a fairly uninteresting husband and two kids in the suburbs of Baltimore. She was saved, as a child, when a homeless, alcoholic man rushed into the street to grab her as an oncoming car rushed toward her. Finn, the alcoholic, left the scene and, in a bizarre twist of fate, met up with some vampire gangsters in the midst of an alcoholic bender, was turned, and returned sober and immortal to the homeless shelter, eventually becoming its respected manager. He also went back to school and became an academic. Campbell falls in love with Finn, and both realize their past association. But Campbell is unwilling to leave her children, as her mother left her. The ending is shockingly abrupt and unsatisfying, but both characters are beautifully crafted, and there are interesting discussions about death, the reason for vampires, feminism, immortality, and the meaning of life.

The Argeneau Vampire series, by Lynsay Sands. This series of light, fun, romantic books can only be described as Jane Austen meets a vampire family. I have read the first nine: *A Quick Bite; Love Bites; Single White Vampire; Tall, Dark & Hungry; A Bite to Remember; Bite Me If You Can; Accidental Vampire; Vampires Are Forever;* and *Vampire, Interrupted.* The Argeneau family lives in Canada; they are lovely, a bit eccentric, and at least hundreds of years old. They are all looking for love, and Marguerite, the mother, spends most of her spare time trying to get all her children married happily. These vampires come from Atlantis and have something called nanos inside their bodies that change them into vampires, but for the last fifty years they have fed only from bagged blood. They have strength and immortality and are not affected by religious symbols or garlic. Being staked hurts, but they can survive. Sunlight makes them need much more blood, but they can go out in the daylight. They have good values, although they are very protective of each other, and they have, perhaps, a reasonable fear of discovery. There are rules for vampires and a council to enforce them. You can have only one child every hundred years. You can sire or turn only one vampire. Finding your true life mate is hard, and that person is usually someone whose mind you can't read, unlike most humans. The biggest flaw in all these books is the formulaic sex. Everyone is gorgeous and hot and the sex is always fabulous, passionate, and intense. There is always a total merging of minds, which makes for perfect orgasms.

A Quick Bite stars Lissiana, a two-hundred-year-old vampire with a phobia about blood, and Greg, a psychologist who treats phobias.

Love Bites concerns Lucian, the brother of Lissiana and the creator of a successful video game. He falls in love with Rachel, a mortal who works in the morgue. She almost dies and is turned when a killer comes for Lucian a second time. Most of the book involves Rachel learning what she now is.

Single White Vampire is about Lucern, who is six hundred years old, rather grumpy, and anti-social. A writer of vampire romances, his editor, Kate, learns what Lucern is, has to steal blood for him, and in the end has to struggle with the choice whether to be turned and live as a life mate with Lucern—all of which is handled with a loving touch.

Tall, Dark & Hungry concerns Bastien Argeneau, who runs the family business. He is more than four hundred years old and a workaholic. Bastien falls in love with Kate's best friend, Terri, and totally changes; he takes her out to museums (he hasn't been to a museum in 120 years) and to street fairs, staying in the shade so he doesn't need more blood. There are funny scenes when Bastien tries food. As usual the sex is too perfect and the end too predictable.

A Bite to Remember has more mystery and suspense and fewer sex scenes. This one involves Vincent, who is many hundreds of years old, runs a theater company, and is totally bored with life. He falls in love with a woman who has a dislike of immortals stemming from a horrible experience with a vampire when she was nineteen. She slowly changes.

In *Bite Me If You Can,* Lucian is thousands of years old and hasn't had sex since Roman times. He is as stodgy and as much of a loner as they come. He is a rogue hunter who hunts those vampires who kill humans and don't obey the rules. He meets Leigh, a vampire bar owner who was turned by a rogue.

The Accidental Vampire features Victor Argeneau, who has to investigate a vampire who has broken the law by advertising for a mate in a newspaper. In fact, Elvi Black, really Ellen Stone, is an accidental vampire, turned by a stranger. Elvi is a sweetie, but because she has gotten most of her information from books and movies, she has spent five years not eating food, thinking she has no reflection, and sleeping in a coffin. When she meets real vampires and learns the truth, she is so excited, she immediately goes grocery shopping and gets a bed. Of course, Elvi and Victor have perfectly timed orgasms, and, of course, he discovers he can't read her and she is his life mate.

Vampires Are Forever concerns Inez Urso, a human employee of Argeneau Enterprises, and Thomas, who helps Bastien search for Marguerite, who has gone missing in the course of some detective work.

Vampire Interrupted is the ninth book in the Argeneau series; it is perhaps the most complex and just might be the best of the lot. After eight books in which Marguerite plays matchmaker, finding life mates for each of her children, it's finally Marguerite's turn.

It's a convoluted plot in which Marguerite is reunited with the life mate that she met and lost in the past. The series goes on, but now that the mom is fixed up, I have definitely had enough.

Insatiable, **by Meg Cabot.** The author of *The Princess Diaries* has written *Insatiable,* which has definite *Dracula* overtones. Meena is a writer for a soap opera in Manhattan. She possesses the psychic ability of knowing when people will die. She meets Lucien, who turns out to be the son of Dracula; she also meets his evil brother Dimitri. She finds herself in the midst of a huge vampire war, involving the two brothers as well as members of a Vatican military force. Lucien is quite lovely as a melancholy and reluctant vampire. Lucien turns into a dragon when he is angry, and there's a bit of King-George-and-the-dragon going on, not to mention Meena's Joan of Arc–like visions. The romantic parts are quite lovely, and the best scenes are when all the horrible soap opera stars and producers turn out to be evil vamps.

The Dark Prince, **by Christine Feehan.** This is the first book in the Dark series, about an ancient race called the Carpathians. And I am afraid I am only going to tell you about the first in the series, unless someone convinces me they get better. Telepathic Raven is traveling in vampire territory, on vacation from arduous work tracking serial killers. She meets Mikhail, the prince of the Carpathians. The Carpathians aren't *exactly* vampires, although they have super strength; can turn into wolves, birds, and mist; and can read minds. They have every vampire quality you can imagine, but they are loyal citizens and even support the Church. They can be killed, but they can live for thousands of years. They feed on blood but do not kill their prey. But, if they are not careful, their dark side can dominate and they can become rogue, killing humans when they feed and forcing them sexually. In other words, they can become real vampires, which the Carpathians must hunt down and kill. The Carpathians are on the verge of going extinct; only males are being born. And if the males live without finding their life mate, they eventually lose the ability to feel and see colors until the mate is found. So far so good.

Mikhail is the dark, unbelievably good-looking prince who has killed many to protect his people. Raven, of course, has a small waist, big boobs, and is perfect. The summary of this book could be as follows: Mikhail: "You will be my life mate, you must obey because I have to protect you." Raven: "I need my freedom," followed by formulaic, lurid sex scene. Repeat several times. Mikhail forcefully takes and gives blood to Raven three times, turning her, so that she will be his life mate, giving her no choice in the matter. After my strong reaction, I went on Amazon to read the citizen reviews. A lot of people like this series, but a substantial minority gave the book only one out of five stars. Part of the problem is that Christine Feehan has written twenty-three (!) Dark series novels in thirteen years and has written more than twenty other novels in the same period. A good editor, slowing down, and less formulaic sex might help.

***Dark Lover,* by J. R. Ward.** This is the first novel in the Black Dagger Brotherhood series. A lot of sex, sex, sex, like so many of these romances, but less violent than Hamilton's Anita Blake novels, and no obsession with S&M. Ah, but it is the first book in the series, so who knows? These are not your gothic vamps. Sunlight does kill them; they are super strong and they can dematerialize. But only the blood of a vampire of the opposite sex can sustain them, and they have to drink only once a month. Otherwise, they eat and drink normally, and none of the other gothic stereotypes apply. Beth has never known her father, Darius, and never knew that he was a powerful and still living vampire; she never knew that she was a half vampire and might go through the transition in her twenties. Her father had asked the most powerful vampire in the Black Brotherhood, Wrath, to help his daughter through the transition, believing his blood would be pure and strong enough. Wrath refuses. But when her father, who has kept watch secretly over her for years, is killed, Wrath becomes Beth's protector, to make sure she will live through the transition. In her previous life, Beth was a reporter on a local upstate New York paper, with various cop friends. But she is protected by Wrath and goes through the change with him. He falls in love with her and they mate. The real forces of darkness in this novel are the lesser, pale humans who hunt vampires and are under the sway of something called the Omega, to whom they have given up their souls. By the end of book one, Wrath and Beth are king and queen and are about to expand and change the Brotherhood. The vampire names are a bit silly—Torhment, Zsadist, Wrath, etc.—and the steamy sex is over the top, but some of the characters are interesting, and Wrath as a powerful but almost blind vampire is an unusual character.

Lothaire, **by Kresley Cole.** When I read this book, I confess that I had no idea what it was about. I saw it on the best-seller list; it is the twelfth book in the Immortals after Dark series, and I hadn't read any of the others. Basically, worlds collide. Ellie is a young, Appalachian tough cookie who seems to be possessed by a demon, Saroya, a death goddess. Lothaire, a vampire, meets Ellie and is bonded, or Blooded; suddenly, after eons he has a heartbeat and thinks Saroya, the demon, is his destined queen, not the mere poor mortal Ellie. He is trying to get a magical ring that will snuff out Ellie's soul so Saroya can use the body and become his queen. To this end he leaves Ellie in prison almost until her execution by lethal injection. He saves her at the last minute. The rest of the book is the story of Lothaire slowly realizing that it is Ellie and not Saroya who is his beloved. Lothaire is arrogant and violent; Saroya is a ruthless killer. When Ellie is with him, Lothaire actually experiences happiness for the first time. This is a dark, complex world, filled with all kinds of supernatural characters. The novel ends without resolution; I guess you have to get the next book. I won't, most probably.

Kiss of Midnight: A Midnight Breed Novel, by Lara Adrian.

This is another romance series that verges into porn with frequent sex scenes with large male members, juices flowing, and multiple orgasms. The protagonists are young. In this series, vampires are an alien species that came to Earth more than a thousand years ago. Only men are vampires. But they mate with human women who stay young through their blood, and who bear children. There is a sign on the women who are breed mates—a teardrop birth mark next to a crescent moon. Lucan is the leader of one group of the Breed, and they are warring with rogue vampires who are becoming stronger. Lucan meets Gabrielle, a photographer, and there is hot sex between them. He pretends he is a cop, after she witnesses a series of brutal rogue murders outside a club. Lucan discovers her mark. He has never mated in his nine hundred years and, although he is determined to protect her, he does not want to mate, despite being drawn to her. There are tons of battles with rogues and the minions they control, until finally, Lucan realizes his true love. These vamps can't be in the sun but are awake during the day and they have quite an honor code. For example, Lucan honors a fallen comrade by being with him in the sun for eight minutes and suffering severe burns. By reading a short few pages of the sequel, I realize that there is something similar here to the Argeneau Vampire books, because the second book is about another warrior who also doesn't want to get hitched when he finds his true mate. Very so-so.

REGIONAL VAMPIRE NOVELS

Authors:

Charlaine Harris, Chloe Neill, Inanna Arthen
(These could all fall under Romance as well.)

NPR HAS A SUMMER SERIES called Crime in the City. Reporters interview authors of crime novels in which the place is as rich a part of the story as the characters. These regional novels— Southern, Chicago, New England—can all claim that kind of status. Anyone who has seen the rich, sultry, two-minute introduction to the HBO series *True Blood*, which can lay a claim to being the best TV introduction of any show I have ever seen, will understand what I am talking about.

The Southern Vampire Mysteries (also known as the Sookie Stackhouse Novels) by Charlaine Harris. Books in this series include *Dead until Dark, Living Dead in Dallas, Club Dead, Dead to the World, Dead as a Doornail, Definitely Dead, All Together Dead, From Dead to Worse, Dead and Gone, Dead in the Family, Dead Reckoning,* and *Deadlocked. A Touch of Dead* contains the complete Stackhouse short stories, and a short story volume, *Many Bloody Returns,* also has a Stackhouse story.

The HBO series *True Blood* is loosely based on the books. The novels take place in Northern Louisiana. Much of the action takes place in two bars, Merlottes and Fangtasia. In this alternate world of today, the Japanese have developed a synthetic form of blood and vampires can "come out" and be legal. Sookie Stackhouse is a mind-reading waitress with some fairy blood, who falls in love with Bill Compton, a vampire who was turned after the Civil War. Sookie cannot read the minds of vampires—which is relaxing, since it is pretty awful to always know what others are thinking. Another vampire, Eric Northman, has a huge role in the books and TV show and also becomes a love interest for Sookie. Later novels involve shapeshifters, werewolves, werepanthers, and fairies. There's lots of political intrigue between the various "supes," or supernaturals, wars between vampire kingdoms and between the fairies, not to mention the complexities between townspeople, the police, the life in Merlotte's bar, and more. One book details the attempt of shapeshifters to come out just like the vampires; another deals with Sookie coming to know her own history and fae side. Some of the later books are not as well written, and the last book of the series, *Dead Ever After,* was hated by hundreds of citizen reviewers, mainly fans of the relationship between Sookie and Eric. But in the end it was inevitable that Sookie would end up not with a vampire but with a supernatural who can be with her in the sunshine she so loves. The HBO television show is a lot darker and more violent than the books.

The Chicagoland Vampires series, by Chloe Neill. This series includes *Some Girls Bite, Friday Night Bites, Twice Bitten, Hard*

Bitten, Drink Deep, Biting Cold, House Rules, and *Biting Bad.* When I came across this series, I totally gobbled it up. The story is about Merit, a twenty-seven-year-old graduate student in medieval literature, living with her friend Mallory, who has a job at an advertising agency. Merit is attacked by a rogue vampire and saved by a master vampire, Ethan, the head of the House of Cadogan. However, to save her, he turns her, and she becomes a vampire who must swear allegiance to his house, one of three Chicago vampire houses. It is not something she wants. She certainly doesn't want to swear an oath of allegiance to the liege, Ethan, whom she finds amazingly attractive but also hates for giving her no choice in the matter of her turning. Throughout this first book, she becomes used to her lot. She ends up training with Catcher, a sorcerer, and finds herself surprisingly strong. She learns martial arts and swordplay. She is talented and becomes the Sentinel, or chief guard, of Cadogan House.

In book two, *Friday Night Bites,* Merit moves in to Cadogan House, while her friend Mallory is trained by Catcher in sorcery. She also has to deal with her super-rich and politically connected Chicago family.

Twice Bitten, the third book in the series, is the best of the three. Merit and Ethan get drawn into the wars between shifters. Mallory and Merit come into their own powers. Ethan and Merit finally get it on. (I love that this series is clearly a romance, but it takes three books until we have any sex.)

Hard Bitten is an unexpected tour de force. By the end, many of the main protagonists are no longer in the picture. We finally learn the truth of Merit's beginnings as a vampire, and we learn more about the political roles of the Mayor and of Merit's father. What's more, a new drug has come into the city that increases the violence of vampires. Its origins and who's behind it are basic themes of the book.

Drink Deep, the fifth book, is complex and has a certain *Buffy* tinge, in that Mallory, like Willow in *Buffy,* goes over to the dark side. We come to understand that magic can be as much of an addiction as alcohol, drugs, or sex. Cadogan House is under receivership by the Greenwich Presidium, and the vampires in the house have to follow horrible rules; they are denied blood, constantly hungry, and not at their best. Vampires are being blamed for supernatural phenomena that are wrecking the city. As a result, humans are pushing for new vampire and supernatural registration laws, shades of *True Blood.* Merit shows her character again and makes decisions that are moral rather than politically advantageous.

Biting Cold involves the continuing struggle to stop Mallory from pursuing evil. In *House Rules,* Cadogan House finally leaves the Greenwich Presidium, threatening the power and financial stability of the house. In *Biting Bad,* there are riots against vampires and supernaturals. One of the vampire houses is almost destroyed. But the riots are a cover; the real plot is more sinister—a medical experiment to rid the world of vampires.

This whole series is fun and compelling. And it sticks with you. One of the best things about the series is its love of Chicago, the sense of place, the sports, the politics, not to mention Merit's love of high-calorie Chicago food. All the characters work well, and the descriptions of Chicago seem spot-on. These vampires are allergic to sunlight and sleep during the day. They are not affected by silver, crosses, or garlic, and they are strong, heal fast, can glamour people, and are immortal unless staked or exposed to the sun. My one criticism of the series: the men are too perfect; there isn't a single shifter or vampire who isn't gorgeous. No nerds? No nice but ugly people? Even Jeff, the computer nerd shifter, seems to have a perfect body. A little more reality in a world with such good characters would be lovely. But the most important thing about this series is this: we have a female vampire who comes to terms with her new life and attempts to deal with an authoritarian hierarchy that she instinctively hates but manages to work within, with honor, loyalty, and hard work. She makes the best she can of one difficult situation after another—difficult people, a difficult family, a rigid structure, a Master, a Presidium, etc., and she still thrives. And the sex is understated and handled with finesse. It has occurred to me to wonder if Neill had a stint in the military. The novels deal with the question of how to keep your individuality amid an authoritarian structure. How, despite these demands, do you keep your basic self-identity, your love of place and people, and your basic sense of humor? How do you continue to thrive? All these questions are dealt with in chapter after chapter, and that's why the series works so well. I list this series among my favorites in "The Best" section.

The Vampires of New England series, by Inanna Arthen: *Mortal Touch* **and** *The Longer the Fall.* *Mortal Touch* is a lovely novel. The basic story is about a woman who is psychically gifted and can "read" people by touching them. She runs a secondhand store in a small New England town. She is asked by a psychologist to investigate a series of nonlethal assaults and comes across a mysterious man who turns out to be a writer but also a moral vampire. A series of incidents and disasters leave a number of people among the undead.

The Longer the Fall is the second book in the Vampires of New England series. It is steeped in ceremonial magic. The protagonist meets up with a fascinating immortal who turns out to be a vampire, and they start on a ceremonial magic quest. The story is very much about unleashing forces that you don't understand with consequences that are unforeseen and tragic. *Mortal Touch* seems more accessible to a general public.

VAMPIRES as OTHER SPECIES, VAMPIRES in SCIENCE FICTION, VAMPIRISM as DISEASE

Authors:

Whitley Strieber, Suzy McKee Charnas, Michael Talbot, Octavia Butler, Robert Matheson, Justin Cronin (*see* Horror), Guillermo Del Toro and Chuck Hogan (*see* Horror), George R. R. Martin, Scott Westerfeld, Dan Simmons, Colin Wilson, Rebecca Rock, Margaret L. Carter, Susan and Clay Griffith (*see* Alternate History)

AROUND THE TIME I was on my 225th vampire novel, I came across an excellent book about vampires in science fiction. *Different Blood: The Vampire as Alien,* by Margaret L. Carter, was published in 2004, so it doesn't include some of the more recent novels and short stories, but it is a fantastic survey of all otherworldly vampires and vampires as other species. The books in this section posit vampires not as demons, or supernatural beings, but simply as another species than human. There are also some novels here about vampirism as a disease, some of them written partly as a response to the AIDS epidemic. The books listed by Cronin, Del Toro, and Hogan definitely fit the vampires-as-disease model, but are reviewed in the Horror section above.

"Food to All Flesh," by Zenna Henderson. Margaret L. Carter, in her book *Different Blood,* alerted me to a wonderful short story, "Food to All Flesh," written in 1953 by the science fiction writer Zenna Henderson. It is totally original and unexpected: a simple story of an alien moral vampire. It's kind of an antidote to that famous *Twilight Zone* episode where the aliens come down with a book that says, "To Serve Man." Padre Manuel is outside a small adobe church when the spaceship comes down. He is almost dizzy when he realizes he is the first human to encounter a being from outer space. A creature comes out; they try to converse; he hands the creature a prayer book. He realizes the creature is hungry. He tries to find something the creature can eat, but the creature regurgitates each thing he gives her. The next morning, after Mass, he tries more things. Nothing works. The creature is a mom, and she brings out her little babies, all so hungry, and nothing works. Then one of the tiny creatures bites him, purrs, and falls asleep. His blood is the first thing that feeds them. The mother creature stares at him a long time, takes all the babies, goes back into the ship, and takes off. End of story. Carter also alerted me to three science fiction vampire stories by Ray Bradbury, written in 1946 and 1947 and published in October Country: "Homecoming," "Uncle Einer," and "The Man Upstairs."

The Hunger, The Last Vampire, **and** ***Lilith's Dream,*** **by Whitley Streiber.** Whitley Strieber has written three vampire novels. The most famous is *The Hunger,* but there are two sequels: *The Last Vampire* and *Lilith's Dream.* His idea was to imagine vampires not as supernatural, but simply a different, stronger, nearly immortal species. The vampire protagonist, Miriam Blaylock, is perhaps so ancient she is Lilith herself. She is truly rapacious, but she just doesn't consider humanity at all. Still, it is much more of a standard horror view of vampires than most of the books considered here.

The Vampire Tapestry, **by Suzy McKee Charnas.** This novel consists of five related stories featuring the mysterious vampire Dr. Edward Weyland. He makes his living as a professor but is an alien species and the last of his kind. The stories are beautifully written. In many ways, Weyland is a cipher; he clearly has no real love of humanity, just a will to survive, but there is poignancy to him as well.

The Delicate Dependency: A Novel of the Vampire Life, **by Michael Talbot.** Whitley Strieber once told me that this was the best vampire novel ever written. Vampires are truly another species in this book, and unbeknownst to humans, they are responsible for preserving much of human culture. Despite this, they consider themselves pretty much above the present human population, whom they don't much care for. It's a very odd, mysterious, and mesmerizing read. One image I will never get out of my mind is a huge vampire banquet; the vampires do not eat, but the aromas of extraordinary foods are enough to satisfy desire. This title is out of print but available from used booksellers.

Fledgling, **by Octavia Butler.** An absorbing and very disturbing novel. The late Octavia Butler was a very talented science fiction writer. The protagonist, Shori, is a half human, half vampire who is a genetic experiment. She is dark skinned (Octavia Butler was African American), and therefore can survive in the daytime. Vampires are definitely another species, living secretly on Earth. Shori appears to be an African American girl of about eleven, but is actually a fifty-three-year-old member of the Ina, a race of vampires that have a symbiotic relationship with humans for sustenance. Shori wakes up injured, her memory impaired, and someone is attacking her family. The book starts out as an exploration of difference, prejudice, and race. But as it goes along there are other hugely important themes such as free will and compulsion in relationships. The human symbionts love being bitten—it is ecstatic and sensual, but it becomes an addiction, and eventually, if they don't have the venom, they can die. There are very disturbing elements in this book's exploration of freedom, and I found myself identifying with the humans much more than the vampires. Some people find the book distasteful because Shori has a sexual relationship with an adult human, and she looks like an eleven-year-old. But she isn't, so I didn't find it a problem.

I Am Legend, **by Robert Matheson.** This 1954 novel is a classic, perhaps the classic vampirism-as-a-disease story. It is a short, apocalyptic science fiction novel, less than a hundred pages. A plague has infected almost everyone—turning them into vampires. Vampirism is a disease; there are dead vampires and living ones. And Robert Neville is the lone survivor. There's lots of science and discussion of genetics, and an odd twist at the end, which turns the whole idea of who is the face of terror and superstition and who is normal on its head. There are many film versions of this story.

Fevre Dream, **by George R. R. Martin.** This fabulous novel, written in the early 1980s, is in my top dozen. It takes place in 1857, involves Abner Marsh, an ugly, fat, hard-eating Mississippi steamboat captain who has lost his dream boat and has fallen on hard times. He is sought out by Joshua York, a vampire with a dream to reunite his species with humanity. He is secretive and can only come out during the night, although he makes several day forays, and at first Marsh is not willing to become his partner. But York promises Marsh a dream boat that could be the fastest on the river. York drinks a blood concoction that drives away the red thirst, so he doesn't have to prey on others. But he is in a fight for leadership with Damon Julian, who is the bloodmaster to a bevy of vampires who feed on slaves and prostitutes, all procured by a human named Sour Billy. Billy has dreams of becoming a vampire for his rewards. But Sour Billy has accepted a lie, since these vampires are a separate species, and humans cannot be turned. These vampires are not affected by crosses, garlic, or silver. You have to behead vampires or shoot them in the brain to kill them. The relationship between Abner and Joshua spans a fair amount of time and the ending is lovely. There are magnificent descriptions of river life and Southern scenery. The novel is haunting, filled with steamboat lore and life on the Mississippi; this is truly a unique vampire novel and I list it among my favorites in "The Best" section.

Peeps, **by Scott Westerfeld.** This young adult novel, written in 2005, is another example of vampirism as a parasitical infection. The protagonist, Cal, is a carrier of a parasite that turns people into a kind of vampire. Ever since he was infected about six months ago, he found himself a carrier and has been working for an organization called Night Watch, an ancient order, older than New York City. The organization hunts down those infected with the parasite. Cal has to find those whom he has infected and, eventually, the woman who infected him. These "peeps," as they are called, or parasite positives, hide in the dark, are cannibals, drink blood, and hate all the things they once loved. So you attack them with the things they used to desire, called anathemas. The peeps feed on people and seem inhuman. But Cal starts to notice that some of those he is after are living on pigeons. He realizes that they can be captured and treated. Cal, as a carrier, has some superpowers, but he can't have sex with anyone, or even kiss them, because he might infect them. In the end he figures out that there are different strains of the parasite, and that those he infected can be cured with simple medicine. An odd and entertaining book that proves the world is never what it seems. Every other chapter in this book is a little scientific exploration of real parasites, some fairly creepy.

Children of the Night, **by Dan Simmons.** A really good book, it is truly unique, one of my favorites, and quite beautifully written. It takes place in 1989, right after the fall of the Romanian dictator Nicolae Ceausescu. It was a time when Romanian orphanages were overflowing with AIDS-infected children living in deplorable conditions. A scientific researcher and epidemiologist, Kate Neuman, goes to Romania to study AIDS-infected babies and comes across Joshua, who has been infected but seems to thrive with blood transfusions. She adopts the baby and takes him home. Suddenly, there are attacks on her and attempts to kidnap the baby, and she discovers that he has this strange little organ that takes up blood. A transfusion every month makes him gloriously healthy, when he was on the point of death. She thinks she has discovered a medical breakthrough with implications for AIDS and medical research. Little does she know that the vampires of Romania still exist, and Joshua is to be their new leader after the death of guess who: Dracula. Vlad Tepes is still alive, just barely, and about to die. The book contains lots of science, adventure, violence, mystery, and death. The descriptions of Romania are wonderful. There is a surprising and very optimistic ending. I list this title among my favorites in "The Best" section.

The Space Vampires, by Colin Wilson. This fascinating but imperfect novel is about alien energy vampires who are discovered by astronauts around 2100 AD. They are able to exchange bodies and suck the vital force out of people while giving them a feeling of sexual and metaphysical ecstasy. Wilson was very taken with metaphysical notions and was a follower of Gurdjieff. In the novel, written in 1976, Olaf Carlsen, the commander of a spaceship, teams up with a criminologist, Dr. Hans Fallada, after a strange encounter with a huge, fifty-mile-long ship. They enter the ship and bring three alien beings back to Earth. The spaceship is extraordinary with huge castle-like structures and semi-nude humanoid creatures in suspended animation. Carlsen and Fallada try to figure out what is happening when the beings are brought to Earth. They appear to have died, but in fact have taken other bodies. They must work fast before the huge ship is entered again with the possibility that more dangerous aliens will be brought to Earth. The experience of having energy drawn is ecstatic, although it kills. Fallada believes that vampirism is part of humanity, and that many people in fact do draw energy from others. The end is very odd and involves two different sets of aliens. A mediocre movie, *Lifeforce,* was based on this book.

Daywalker, **by Rebecca Rock.** A strange book, *Daywalker* works only as the first of a series. Although written in 2007, I don't see any sequel. It takes place on a very human-like world. The protagonist is Jesse, whose real name is Adam. Superficially an engineering student at a university, with werewolf roommates, he is secretly half Landian (a planet about to be at war with humans) and half vampire. But he keeps his vampire side under control and secret. The Landians (who have incredible powers) killed his parents and Jesse has been trained in a Special Forces unit for the coming war with the Landians. Meanwhile he wears a cross to protect himself, for he knows that if vampires knew he was a hybrid, they would kill him, because he can walk in the day. He takes plasma pills to prevent bloodlust. The first part of the book involves his relationship with his roommates, the local werewolf pack, and various vampires. Then he is called to battle as the war begins. A huge Landian ship destroys a whole planet, and the humans and the Special Forces unit attempt to fight back. Their weapons are empathy, telepathy, and "syms" that are implanted that give the fighters special qualities and healing powers. The book ends with the war in process. We never find out what happens with the people Jesse left behind at the university. We do know that during the battle he goes all out to avenge the death of his parents; he kills blindly and experiences bloodlust for the first time. Many threads are left hanging, so the book is unsatisfying.

Dark Changeling and _Child of Twilight,_ by Margaret L. Carter. I mentioned Carter and her book _Different Blood: The Vampire as Alien,_ but she has also written a number of vampire novels. I was not disappointed in _Dark Changeling._ It's well written except that Carter, or the printer, has a distracting habit of hyphenating hundreds of normal words. Written in 1999, the story is about a forty–year-old psychiatrist, Roger Darvell, who has a dark secret, bloodlust and drinking from people; he also has the ability to cure his patients more easily than others, by putting them in a trance. He slowly discovers at a late age, near forty, that he is a half vampire, with many vampire abilities, except he cannot change into other forms. He also has no problem with crosses and goes to church, although he hates garlic and can stand only some sunlight. He is a rationalist and skeptic and can't really believe he is a vampire. He eventually moves to the Baltimore area where his new partner, Britt, is totally fascinated as she discovers the truth about him and falls in love. He drinks from her and their union is ecstatic. There are many sex scenes in the novel, and they are done quite well. Vampires are a separate species in this world. They have an estrus cycle; male vampires do not ejaculate except during those rare times they can make a woman vampire pregnant. Meanwhile a rogue vampire killer is on the loose and Roger, our protagonist, is trying to find him.

Child of Twilight is the sequel to *Dark Changeling*. Dr. Roger Darvell is still with Britt, but he has also fathered a child, Gillian, with a vampire named Juliette, since vampires are in danger of not reproducing. Now, Camille, the sister of the vampire killer in the previous book, is determined to have her revenge on Roger, for the murder of her brother. Camille forces a blood bond with Gillian and tries to teach her to be a ruthless killer who believes humans are useful only as food. Gillian is a young, frightened hybrid who needs to find safety and wise teachers. The book also asks the question whether there can ever be total trust between humans and vampires.

SUPERNATURAL FANTASY

Authors:

Carrie Vaughn, Sergei Lukyanenko, Kim Harrison,
Billie Sue Mosiman, L. J. Smith, Christopher Pike,
RaShelle Workman, K. P. Ambroziak

ALTHOUGH SUPERNATURAL and fantasy elements run throughout many of the novels in this annotated list, fantasy, dreams, and the supernatural dominate in these novels. I am putting several other urban paranormal fantasy series in a separate category called Vampire Hunters Since Buffy.

The Kitty Norville series, by Carrie Vaughn. I start this section with the Kitty Norville novels by Carrie Vaughn: *Kitty and the Midnight Hour, Kitty Goes to Washington, Kitty Takes a Holiday, Kitty and the Silver Bullet, Kitty and the Dead Man's Hand, Kitty Raises Hell, Kitty's House of Horrors, Kitty Goes to War,* and *Kitty's Big Trouble.* Although these books star a werewolf, not a vampire, they have lots of vampire politics and intrigue. They could easily be in the detective, crime-fighting genre, and even in the romance genre, but Kitty is constantly fighting supernatural forces.

In the first book, *Kitty and the Midnight Hour,* Kitty is a DJ in Denver, and a secret werewolf. She turns her typical music show into a call-in show where she deals with the supernatural and gives serious counseling advice. She ends up revealing herself as a werewolf, which brings her into lots of trouble, partly because her pack is not happy about her show. She is not dominant, but she slowly gains strength and has to prove herself to Carl, the pack leader, and to Meg, his partner who hates her, and to TJ, who is the second dominant in the pack and her good friend. Meanwhile, she has to help solve a crime committed by a rogue werewolf who is murdering women. She also must deal with the police, who are not sure what to think of her, and she also has to negotiate with the local vampire family. In the end, she leaves the pack after a horrible death.

In the second book, *Kitty Goes to Washington,* Kitty is now alone, without her pack, and she has to do her show from different locations because she is no longer welcome by the werewolves in Denver. She is called to testify before a Senate committee that is investigating the paranormal—hearings that have McCarthy over-tones. She finds herself welcomed by the vampire mistress of the city, Alette, who, although aloof, old, world-weary, and very upper class, turns out to be a good ally by the end. Kitty finds a club that caters to werewolves and there she finds an association that is much more modern, forward thinking, and forgiving than a pack. She meets a were-hunter and his lawyer and together they take down a preacher who has formed a false cult, convincing werewolves and vampires that he can cure them. At one point, Kitty is captured and forced to change during the full moon on TV, quite a scene. Now she is really "out."

Kitty Takes a Holiday has no vampires, but it does involve Cormac, the hunter who helped her find Ben, her lawyer. Ben is bitten by a werewolf and becomes her partner in the rest of the books.

In *Kitty and the Silver Bullet,* Kitty has to deal with both werewolf and vampire politics. Kitty ends up a pawn in a complex political game by a very powerful vampire named Mercedes.

Kitty and the Dead Man's Hand doesn't quite work as well as the others. Kitty and Ben go to Las Vegas to get married. Kitty comes to watch Balthazar and his tiger act, which she quickly realizes is connected to a sinister cult that deals in werewolf sacrifice. There is way too much demonic and supernatural stuff in this novel for my taste.

Kitty returns to Denver in *Kitty Raises Hell,* only to find that the New Moon Bar, her attempt with Ben to create a werewolf club like the one in D.C., has been defaced and there is a new threat: Djinn, a fire genie. In the midst of all this, a mysterious vampire called Roman turns up, telling Kitty he will protect her if she swears loyalty to him, which she refuses to do. He is a two-thousand-year-old vampire who is involved in a power play lasting over centuries. Meanwhile, after a pack member dies, Kitty's authority is questioned. All these threads come together in a quite satisfying read.

Kitty is invited to be on a reality TV show in *Kitty's House of Horrors,* along with Odysseus Grant, an amazing magician from Las Vegas, several psychics, a werewolf, a wereseal, two vampires, and a total skeptic. They are put in a house in Montana, away from civilization, with no cell phone service. It starts normally, with the kind of gossip you would expect in a reality show, but Tina, the psychic, picks up serious hate flowing around them. Suddenly, they wake to find four people dead, all the show producers have disappeared, and all the equipment is gone. Plus, the house is booby-trapped. It is all a setup; the three producers are really right-wing nuts and hunters of supernatural beings.

In *Kitty Goes to War,* we learn that some werewolves, trained as Special Forces in Afghanistan, were developed into special killers. But after the pack leader died, the rest became unmanageable. Called in to help, Kitty convinces both the military and the paranormal investigators that two of the wolves are salvageable, and she convinces the military to let her bring them into the pack on a full moon. It doesn't work out well, and magical weather complicates the issue. It's never clear if Roman—his Long Game—is behind it all.

In *Kitty's Big Trouble,* Kitty takes up the battle with Roman and the Long Game. She is called to San Francisco by the eight-hundred-year-old vampire Anastasia to rescue a treasure that can replicate anything, to keep it out of the hands of Roman, who wants to use it to create an army beholden to him.

What I like about this series is how Kitty changes from a vulnerable, submissive wolf to an independent, strong leader. I like that vampires and werewolves live in the real world and have real jobs, and there is humor.

Nightwatch and **Daywatch, by Sergei Lukyanenko.** Both novels are set in Moscow in the late '90s, after the fall of the Soviet Union. This is the story of the Others, a group of formerly human, supernatural beings who fight for light or dark. There is the Nightwatch, who fight for the light, and the Daywatch, witches and vampires, who fight for the dark. They have a treaty and maintain a balance (something like old Cold War politics).

If one gets out of hand, the other side gets an advantage to create balance again, but as the story gets deeper, these categories shift and nothing is what it seems.

In *Nightwatch,* the hero is Anton Gorodetsky, a midlevel magician and Nightwatch agent who falls in love with Swetlana, or Sweta, who is being groomed to be a powerful sorceress. This is a dark urban fantasy, but set in Moscow, and you do feel you are there. In the end it is very much about free will and determinism, and who decides. There are moments when the forces of light seem responsible for the darkest of ideas—fascism and communism—and the dark forces, being libertarian, seem concerned only about individualism and the freedom to do what they want. There's a constant tug between helping humanity and turning to evil.

Daywatch, the second book, is more coherent, and the characters are more compelling. The first section involves a dark witch, Alisa, who has lost her powers and goes to a resort in the Crimea and a pioneer camp to restore them. She meets Igor and falls in love with him, not realizing that he is a light magician sent to the camp for the same reason. It is all part of a plot by the head of Moscow Daywatch that doesn't end well. The second part involves another vast plot and a dark Other, who finds himself compelled to come to Moscow and is not what he appears to be. The third section involves a tribunal in Prague that judges whether Igor is guilty of murder. This all takes place near the year 2000, and there is a bit too much about the apocalypse and the birth of the Messiah. But the characters are interesting. The writing is quite lovely at times, and there is this feel of Russia made more palpable by the constant use of poetry and verse from Russian music groups.

***Dead Witch Walking,* by Kim Harrison.** This could probably also go in the Detective Vampire Fiction section. It is the first of a series. It starts out fairly formulaic, but some of the characters are interesting. There are Inderlanders and humans in this world, after something called the great Turn. There are two different policing groups, the IS, where Rachel works as a Runner and takes down people who do illegal things—these include vampires and witches who are into the black arts. There is also a human police force. Rachel is being downgraded, gets worse and worse assignments, and is finally let go. Morgan is a very successful living vamp—that means she will become undead when she actually dies but she already has many of the powers of a vampire: strength, speed, and the ability to compel. She also works for the IS and wants to leave, but is considered very valuable. The two women decide to team up as a private agency, and there is a third partner, a pixie named Jenks. The rest of the novel is a somewhat predictable series of attempts on Rachel's life and Rachel's attempts to take down evil doers. There are some surprises and some interesting scenes between Morgan, a very appealing but somewhat scary vampire, and Rachel. Not bad all and all.

***Red Moon Rising, Malachi's Moon,* and *Craven Moon,* by Billy Sue Mosiman.** This is a trilogy of rather unique vampire books, and I enjoyed them. There are three different kinds (nations) of vampires in these stories, and they are chosen in the dream world, depending on their spirit: predators, naturals (who live as humans), and cravens. The first book is about the coming of age of Dell, a natural, and the last two are about her son, Malachi, a dhampir, half human and half vampire.

The Night World series, by L. J. Smith. There are three short novels in the first book: *Secret Vampire, Daughters of Darkness,* and *Spellbinder.* They all involve vampires, witches, and shapeshifters that live in the regular world but have a secret society with ironclad laws. Smith, who also wrote the Vampire Diaries series, has many more short novels in this Nightworld series.

The Thirst series, by Christopher Pike. This series includes three stories, "The Last Vampire," "Black Blood," and "Red Dice," all bundled into volume one of what is clearly already a four-volume series. Sita, her original name, or Alisa, as she calls herself now, is a five-thousand-year-old vampire. She was made by the first vampire, Yaksha, a kind of demon, way back when. She is nocturnal, but can function in the sun, more so now that she is so old. She has lived in many societies. She met Krishna, the god she speaks to and thinks and dreams about during the book. Although there are a number of Indian references, Alisa is a blond, blue-eyed, petite girl who looks about nineteen or younger; she is ridiculously strong, and—like Nathaniel Cade in those presidential vampire thrillers—she is very jaded, kills with ease, and falls in love too easily as well. The entire saga is told in a first-person narrative that doesn't work very well. This is the story of a vampire with less-than-human qualities, with super strength, yet not a real monster, someone who can sometimes love and take moral positions. She falls in love with several people, including one man, after she kills his detective father; she also has feelings for a high school nerd—very brilliant—who is the only person to whom she reveals herself. There is a lack of depth in all the relationships, and Alisa, herself, is pretty one-dimensional.

The Blood and Snow series, by RaShelle Workman. This young adult supernatural fantasy purports to be four short novellas, but is really only four sections of a 232-page book. But the story, while having some odd aspects, is quite gripping. It's your typical young teen who doesn't see herself as beautiful, is klutzy, and comes into awesome powers. Snow White—yes, that is her name—has a best friend named Cindy (short for Cinderella). She lives with her father and her stepmother, who has a Disney fetish. There are Disney characters all over the house, but the parents are wealthy and not around much. Her "real" family is next door: a whole wonderful gaggle of adopted boys, taken in by a religion professor who is called Professor Pops. Very soon, in a dream realm filled with all kinds of supernatural creatures, Snow is bitten and begins her change into a revenant. She finds out that she is being groomed to be the next body for the evil vampire Queen. Meanwhile, Snow starts desiring blood, drinks a special tea to stave off bloodlust, and begins desiring two different young men. The family of boys and their father turn out to know all about the supernatural; they are warriors of sorts, with an amazing museum of the supernatural in their basement. They start training her in swordplay and instruct her in the supernatural world as she approaches her sixteenth birthday. The first four novellas end with a horrid tragedy, a real cliffhanger, and it is not clear where Snow is going on her vampire journey.

The Fifth Empire: The Journal of Vincent du Maurier, **by K. P. Ambroziak.** The story takes place in the year 2052, in a world overrun by the "living dead," or Zombies. A bite causes both humans and vampires to become infected and turn into these almost non-sentient creatures. A small group of vampires is struggling to survive, as the human blood supply dwindles. One of the leading vampires has a plan to save both species. But his scientific experiments to inoculate against infection have so far led nowhere. Eventually the team, growing smaller by the minute, rescues a pregnant woman. Despite the growing weakness of the vampires and their bloodlust, they protect her—they believe she holds the key to repopulating the Earth. These vampires are strong and can be in the sun after seventy-five years, and none of the gothic myths apply. They make their home in a cathedral for a while. By the end of this first book in a series, only two vampires and two humans remain, including the pregnant woman, but they have found a partial solution to the Zombie threat. Though it's slow in the beginning, I found myself gripped by the story halfway through and raced to the end. A sequel, *The Fifth Empire: The Harvest of Vincent de Maurier,* has just been released. It continues the saga of the vampire Vincent De Maurier's attempt to save humanity by protecting the pregnant human, Evelyn, and her baby from the Zombie threat. It's dark and violent, but gripping.

ALTERNATE HISTORY

Authors:

Kim Newman, Chelsea Quinn Yarbro, Sarah Jane Stratford, Terence Taylor, Alaya Johnson, Susan and Clay Griffith

THERE ARE TONS of novels that add vampires to historical settings: vampires allying with the Nazis, vampires in the Roaring Twenties, vampires on the *Hindenburg*, vampires in ancient Rome, you name it. Many of these cross with other genres. For example, you could categorize George R. R. Martin's *Fevre Dream* as a kind of alternate history of life on the Mississippi River in the 19th century—I discuss it in the Vampires as Other Species section.

The Anno Dracula series, by Kim Newman. Kim Newman has written the classic series of alternate vampire histories: *Anno Dracula, The Bloody Red Baron, Judgment of Tears: Anno Dracula 1959,* and, most recently, *Anno Dracula 1976–1991: Johnny Alucard. Anno Dracula* could have been a really good novel; it is praised by reviewers as one of the best vampire novels ever, but it has several failings. The idea is brilliant: imagine how different the world would be if Dracula existed and had not been killed by Van Helsing. The book takes place three years after the Stoker novel.

Dracula is in power in Victorian London, has married Queen Victoria, and become the real power behind the throne. Vampires are turned easily, and newborn vamps are all over the place. Turning is seen by many as the only way to achieve power. There is a huge division in society between the alive and the undead, including resistance movements. The world is populated by warms, newborns, and some elders, including Dracula, his brutal Carpathian Guard, and a few others, including the best character Newman ever developed: Geneviève Dieudonné, a vampire born in the 15th century from a different bloodline. This character, or a version of her, is found in previous novellas and short stories by Newman. This is a world characterized by a brutal lack of freedom. People are impaled on stakes by Vlad Tepes and his guards. Many are in concentration camps or have been killed, including Sherlock Holmes, Oscar Wilde, and Gilbert of Gilbert and Sullivan. Renfield and Van Helsing are dead, the latter impaled on a stake outside the palace. Vampire prostitutes not only give sex but also sell their blood for a shilling. The vampires come from different bloodlines and those who come from Dracula are quite tainted. Newborns can't be in the sun, but the elders can, and their need for blood lessens with age. Most, but not all, do not reflect in mirrors. The story involves looking for the murderer of several vamp prostitutes. But the main plot involves Charles Beauregard, a "warm" and an intelligence agent for the Crown, and Geneviève. Both attempt to find the killer. There is a fascinating mix of politics and intrigue. It could have been great. Unfortunately, the writing is often poor and the characters lack depth. The relationship between Charles and Geneviève could have been drawn with more power and passion. Many of the other characters are simply afterthoughts.

In the second book, *The Bloody Red Baron*, Newman rewrites World War I. Dracula has teamed up with the Kaiser and is leading the German forces, and all the pilots are vampires. German medical experimentation has created shapeshifters who have become armed giant bats and are more powerful than the British pilots. We meet Charles Beauregard, once again, and Kate, a vampire journalist. Edwin Winthrop, a rare warm-blooded pilot, fights the Red Baron and also has a relationship with Kate that is quite lovely. In fact, the writing in this book is better and the relationships deeper. Also, there is a surprising appearance of Edgar Allan Poe, on the German side, writing a book about the Red Baron. The British, the French, and the Americans seem to stave off the Germans by the end, but Dracula survives to reappear in the third book, *Judgment of Tears: Anno Dracula 1959*.

Charles Beauregard is still alive, although dying. Geneviève is taking care of him. Dracula is living on the outskirts of Rome and is about to marry a vampire named Asa Vajda of Moldavia. Kate Reed, the journalist turned vampire, is also there, as are a cast of new characters. There are a series of murders of vampire elders by someone called the Crimson Executioner, and there is a powerful goddess of Rome, who seems to pull the strings. Although the ending is weak, there are interesting allusions to Gore Vidal, Orson Welles, and Fellini; there are many imaginative ideas: blood gelatos, vampires with sunglasses on motorcycles, "warms" with spigots in their necks at parties so vampires can have tiny sips. I give it an A for imagination, but a C for the writing.

A fourth book in the series came out in 2013, *Anno Dracula 1976–1991: Johnny Alucard*. It takes place during Francis Ford Coppola's *Dracula* movie and Andy Warhol's New York. It's an over-the-top, star-studded world and concerns the resurrection of Dracula after his death in the 1950s. The Irish vampire Kate Reed and Newman's best character, Geneviève Dieudonné, are both here, but also Orson Welles and assorted movie stars and rock musicians. Films and rock songs from the late '70s and '80s are reimagined, but much of the novel left me cold except for the chapters involving Kate and Geneviève, the two vampire women who have been great characters in all Newman's books.

The Vampire Geneviève series, by Jack Yeovil (pen name of Kim Newman). I would never put this volume in alternate history; it belongs more in fantasy, but it involves the wonderful character in the Kim Newman series above, Geneviève. This volume contains the four Vampire Geneviève novels: *Drachenfels, Beasts in Velvet, Geneviève Undead,* and *Silver Nails.* But I confess I skimmed the last two. It all takes place in the very Germanic and medieval world of Warhammer, the same world as the RPG game. But while Geneviève could be a fabulous vampire character, she doesn't have a huge place in these novels, so it's mostly violent action. There is little character development, just hints of possibility. I got bored, and by the end of the second book I was skimming. The first book, *Drachenfels,* is probably the best, since it revolves around actors, a bizarre play, and many supernatural characters. The ending is surprising and unexpected, but I quickly tired of the whole Warhammer world.

Hôtel Transylvania, The Palace, and Blood Games, by Chelsea Quinn Yarbro. These are three historical novels in the Saint-Germain Cycle—she has written at least twenty of them, but I have not had a chance to get to the others yet. All involve the Comte de Saint-Germain, a moral vampire. *Hôtel Transylvania* is the first book of a series that goes through a vast number of historical periods. The books do not have to be read in order. This book takes place in Paris in 1743, in the time of Louis XV. Saint-Germain has been alive since before Christ, several thousand years. He can walk in the daylight if he wears earth from his native land in his shoes, and he must sleep on native earth. He needs blood from willing donors, but, even more, he needs emotional attachment and is exceedingly lonely. He is strong, but not invincible. In this book he meets and reveals himself to a woman, Olivia, and he changes her into a vampire. She appears in other books.

The Palace is the second book in the series. It takes place in Florence during the end of the reign of the Medicis and is filled with art and historical characters like Botticelli and da Vinci. Saint-Germain comes to Florence, builds his own palazzo with secret rooms for his alchemy, and falls in love with Donna Estasia. The novel details the death of Lorenzo de' Medici and the rise of the renegade priest Savonarola. He starts by destroying the city's art, burning paintings, and later sends heretics to the stake, unleashing a reign of terror. Saint-Germain takes the name of Francesco Ragoczy and he saves Estasia by turning her into a vampire and rescuing her from the flames. The horrors of religious fanaticism are well explored and the writing is lovely. I list this title among my favorites in "The Best" section.

Blood Games is brilliantly written, but it is overly obsessive and filled with violence, political corruption, torture, and horror. It takes place in Rome during the time of Nero and the emperors who followed him, so the violence and horror are understandable. The period is 65 AD and there is incredible detail about Roman life, games, art, food, and slavery. It's hard to imagine a nastier place. Ragoczy, our several-thousand-year-old vampire, is a wealthy foreigner, who has many slaves, chariots, and animals to put into the arena, but he has to walk a fine line to avoid suspicion. He falls in love with the wife of a senator, and finds that he is overwhelmed by his feelings for her. This is Atta Olivia Clemens, who is later turned by him. But in Rome she is almost enslaved by her senator husband, who forces her to have brutal sex with various gladiators while he watches. When Ragoczy and the senator become enemies, Ragoczy finds himself in mortal danger. Olivia cannot leave her husband because he has threatened the rest of her family. Ragoczy's humanity is in total contrast to the lack of humanity of the actual humans in Rome. I got sucked in by the end, and it made me want to journey with Olivia and Saint-Germain into other times.

The Midnight Guardian, by Sarah Jane Stratford. This novel puts vampires in Nazi Germany. There are a group of millennial vampires in England. More than a thousand years old, they are stronger than ordinary vampires, and they are determined to take out the Nazis. It begins as revenge against hunters that have killed all the vampires in Europe. But the vampires come to realize the battle is about more than their revenge; there is a need to save humanity. The main character is wonderful. Brigit, or Brigantia, is a millennial vampire who has actual fire inside her; she has a tormented, dark past, but she has found herself melting through a deep love relationship with Eamon, a formerly Jewish man, now a vampire eight hundred years old. He seems to have a soul, or at least half of one, and is still filled with guilt at his predation. Brigit takes on the task of saving Jewish children. Five of the strongest millennials go to take out the Nazis but the Nazis have teamed up with German and Irish vampire hunters and are stronger than expected. Several millennials do not survive. One of the best parts of the book is the coming together of Brigit with a great Jewish vampire hunter and his children. These are classic vampires in that they can be staked and turn to dust and must avoid the sun. There are some odd and confusing parts of the book but also charming characters, like a great musician who can sing across distances, even across countries, and can get Brigit's heart to beat, saving her from discovery.

A Vampire Testament Trilogy, by Terence Taylor. *Bitemarks* is the first novel in this trilogy by Terence Taylor. Although much of the action takes place in an urban noir New York City during eleven days in 1987, there are flashbacks to the '30s, the '60s, the *Hindenburg* disaster, and many other historical moments. There is a whole underground vampire world in New York City with politics and violence. A human couple, connected to the art world, has decided to write a book on vampires. Meanwhile, a dangerous vampire baby has gotten loose and a sadistic older vampire is wreaking revenge every seven years on a human family, just because he can. All these stories come together by the end. Well written, but a bit too gory for my taste.

Taylor's second effort, *Blood Pressure,* is much better. There is less violence and more nuance and character development. It takes place twenty years later in 2007, with flashbacks to the '20s, the '30s, the Harlem Renaissance, and Zora Neale Hurston. Lori and Steven, the couple who wrote the vampire book in the first novel, have separated, but are on the point of reconciliation. Christopher, the demon baby in the first novel, has become human, through a crazy explosion at the end of the first book. He has returned to New York as a young man to figure out his origins. His body contains an elixir with amazing properties that can turn several vampires into immortal day creatures and others into human beings. There's lots of political conniving in the novel, including a secret vampire society in New York called The Veil. Taylor says he wrote *Blood Pressure* easily, unlike the first book, and it shows. The plot is intricate and the characters are quite wonderful. You find yourself sympathizing with all kinds of characters, even those with an evil past, like a vampire psychiatrist who now does good therapy and feeds without killing.

Moonshine **and** ***Wicked City,*** **by Alaya Johnson.** *Moonshine* is a lovely book that takes place in the 1920s in a dystopian New York City where vampires make up one-fifth of the population. There are other supernatural types including Amir, a djinn, or genie, that the human protagonist (known as Zephyr, or the vampire suffragette) falls in love with, but it's a tormented relationship. Zephyr is the daughter of demon hunters, but she spends most of her time teaching in a school for immigrants and supernaturals and doing other good works. The world includes mafia-like vampire drug lords and a blood drug called Faust. In this world vampires can't drink alcohol without hurting themselves and they get their blood from blood banks. The book takes on prejudice and anti-immigrant sentiment. It takes place five years after women have gained the vote, and there are some lovely characters, including a journalist and a child who has been turned. And in the midst of all this, we have some real history: Mayor Jimmy Walker is a character in the book; there are speakeasies, and a few parties that F. Scott Fitzgerald might well have written about.

Wicked City is the sequel to *Moonshine.* In an era of Prohibition, Zephyr is part of a campaign against the drug Faust, along with Elspeth, a vampire. It's a very hot summer and police start investigating Zephyr for the crime of saving an underage vampire, Judah. In this world, underage vampires are killed because they are too young to be trusted with self-control. Zephyr sent Judah to Montana where her parents live. Meanwhile, Amir, the djinn who brought Faust to the city, is in an increasingly complex relationship with Zephyr, and she wants to get out of her bond with him. Meanwhile, she is accused of a series of vampire murders, and there is a startling revelation at the end. The book is actually lovely and less complicated than the description would make it seem.

The Vampire Empire series by Susan and Clay Griffith. It's hard to know whether to call the Vampire Empire series alternate history, fantasy, romance, or what it has often been dubbed, vampire steampunk. These vampires are also a separate species. A galley of *The Greyfriar* arrived as a freebie in my office and I was captivated. It's a kind of steampunk alternate universe with gas-based flying ships, a steam- and gas-based technology, and unusual weapons. Vampires have conquered many lands. Vampires are tall, thin, and pale and can fly. But they are parasites who have no human culture; they do not read or write, although they can mimic humanity quite well. They do show in mirrors, they do have babies, and they live for about eight hundred years. In the lands they control they keep human herds off of which they feed. They do not do well in the heat, and so humans have moved to hot lands, where they still rule—in Africa and South and North America. The vampire clans and kingdoms rule Europe and are headquartered in London. Adele is a princess and heir to Equatoria—headquartered in Alexandria (it still has a great library) and is about to wed Senator Clark, the leader of the war against vampires in America. But she is captured by vampires and saved by a mysterious human who is always masked and is called Greyfriar. The first volume of the trilogy is the story of Adele and Greyfrier and how they come together, fight, fall in love, and begin to trust each other. Adele has some supernatural powers that she is just beginning to learn to control. I got hooked on this one. I would really be a spoiler if I told you more.

Book two, *The Rift Walker,* is complex; Adele is about to be married to Senator Clark, and the wedding is almost finalized, when, realizing she is in mortal danger from a plot against her and her father, Greyfriar comes and abducts her. She goes with him to a kingdom in Africa where he almost dies but survives. Meanwhile her teacher, Mamoru, a geomancer, realizes Adele's powers are extraordinary and she can ultimately make the earth rise up and kill vampires. She does this in the service of the African King Msiri, destroying almost every vampire attacking Msiri's forces. Meanwhile plots are afoot, by both vampires and humans, to bring down Adele's reign. This volume is not quite as powerful as the first book; there is less time spent on relationships, and more on war.

In book three, the finale, *The Kingmakers,* there are countless plots and intrigues. Empress Adele has launched a battle against the vampire clans of the North, but the battle is not going well and thousands are slaughtered. Mamoru, her powerful geomancy instructor, realizes that Adele's power of geomancy is so great that she could end the vampire threat. But Adele begins to question the morality of this. Vampires ordinarily don't feel pain, but this power burns and can kill them horribly. Mamoru, who lost his family to vampires, is so obsessed with ending their rule that he is determined to force Adele to bring about the destruction of all vampires, even though it will mean her own death. Although some of the steampunk engineering and battle details left me cold, I could read more.

VAMPIRE HUNTERS SINCE BUFFY

Authors:

Laurell K. Hamilton, L. A. Banks, Faith Hunter, Patricia Briggs, Ilona Andrews, Nancy A. Collins

I THOUGHT LONG AND HARD about what to call this section: I almost wanted to call it Vampire Porn, since there is so much sex, violence, and torture in the books by Hamilton and Banks. Both heroines start out as vampire hunters, and just like *Buffy*, things become more complex. They are also kick-ass women, who do all the things men usually do in adventure novels and thrillers. But once you add Briggs and Hunter and other authors who have written about vampire slayers, this genre becomes more nuanced, and the sex is much more understated. One could take all these authors, add Carrie Vaughn, Chloe Neill, and several others and simply put them in the category "urban supernatural fantasy," which many people do. Many of these series are huge best-sellers.

The Anita Blake: Vampire Hunter series by Laurell K. Hamilton. This series includes the books *Guilty Pleasures, The Laughing Corpse, Circus of the Damned, The Lunatic Cafe, Bloody Bones, The Killing Dance, Burnt Offerings, Blue Moon, Obsidian Butterfly,* and *Narcissus*

in Chains. There are another dozen, but I have only read the first ten. Some of these novels are as long as seven hundred pages and many of them reach the level of porn; it's a kind of R-rated *Buffy*. Anita Blake is a gun-toting, knife-wielding vampire executioner, whose day job is as an "animator" raising zombies from the dead. Why would you do that, you may ask. So people can question their ancestors, for example: "What did you really mean by that in your will?"

In the first book, *Guilty Pleasures,* Anita is a fairly prudish and religious young woman who has had sex only once—with her college fiancée—who then left her. She is a Catholic who would never get close to a vampire. By book ten, *Narcissus in Chains,* Blake has changed her religion to Episcopalian, and she is having sex with two vampires, including the remarkable Jean-Claude, a beautifully drawn character, as well as the Ulfric, or king of the local werewolf pack, not to mention several wereleopards. She is becoming more powerful and less human with each book, gaining many magical, vampire, and werewolf abilities. It's totally over the top with sex and violence, including S&M, even torture, more so with each book. But Hamilton has fascinating characters and unusual relationships. It's kind of like watching a car wreck; you can't turn your eyes away.

The Vampire Huntress Legend series, by L. A. Banks. The late L. A. Banks wrote a dozen Vampire Huntress books before she died. I have read the first three: *Minion, The Awakening,* and *The Hunted.* L. A. Banks is an African American writer, and this series is kind of Def Poetry Jam and rap music plus vampires. The heroine is African American, and there is a kind of Khemetic/Egyptian connection in the series and a sense of black culture throughout. Damali, the heroine, is a Neteru—someone born very rarely with an ability to fight vampires and demons. She is just coming into her own, turning twenty-one in the first book. There is this short period of fertility when master vampires want to mate with Neterus. I am not sure this idea really works. Meanwhile the vampire council is fighting its own war with a rogue vampire named Nuit who has allied with demons. Damali is a musician who has a group that plays at clubs, but the group is also a team of guardians who fight vampires. There is a rival music group that is very connected to the dark side, and a Latino love of her life, Carlos, who also figures deeply in the books. Think of Anita Blake, but with more street wisdom. Unfortunately, the writing is uneven and flawed.

In *The Awakening,* Damali comes to realize how compromised her boyfriend is; it's not clear whether he will side with good or evil. The third book is the most interesting of the three. Damali and Carlos reunite, but Damali has to fight a twisted were-jaguar from the Amazon who was the victim of colonial oppression. By the end of book three, Carlos is on the vampire council, and he and Damali are still lovers. Some of the writing is weak, but the series allows you to enter a poetic, rap/ghetto world. Many African American writers of vampire fiction—Octavia Butler, Alaya Johnson, Terence Taylor—do not write about a specifically black culture. Banks does.

The Jane Yellowrock series, by Faith Hunter. This series, including the books *Skinwalker* and *Blood Cross,* is one of the most interesting post-*Buffy* vampire slayer series. Jane Yellowrock is a professional vampire killer for hire, but what makes her unusual is that she is part Cherokee and a supernatural herself, a skinwalker, perhaps the last of her kind. She is able to shapeshift into various animals. She also carries a beast within her—a mountain lion, with his or her own thoughts. Shapeshifting is complex. She eats huge amounts of raw meat and hunts live prey when she shifts. She also uses rituals, sweats, and ceremonies to center and gain strength. The book takes place in New Orleans, and vampires in this world are rogue for their first ten years and must be chained. They only regain their memories and learn control slowly. Jane is originally hired by Katie, a very old vampire who runs a whorehouse; she ends up meeting complex characters, humans, vampires, blood servants, and even blood slaves. Previously she had never met a "civilized vamp," and she has to reorder some of her perceptions.

The second book, *Blood Cross,* is quite well written and involves an attempt by vampires to use witch blood and the sacrifice of witch children to lessen the time newly created vampires are rogue. The vampires seem to have their own religion, seeing themselves as cursed from the time of Judas's betrayal of Jesus. It's a more subtle use of religion than the vampire religion of Lilith worship (totally over the top) that has been central in recent seasons of *True Blood.* The characters, including Leo, Master Vampire of the city, are well drawn, and the romantic element comes on slowly. After Hamilton and Banks, it's a relief.

The Mercy Thompson series, by Patricia Briggs. Briggs has written more than six books featuring Mercy Thompson, an auto mechanic and a walker. Unlike skinwalkers who can turn into the beasts they have some physical connection with, Mercy turns into one animal—a coyote—whenever she desires. Brought up by werewolves, she is fast, but not as strong as they are. The novels take place in the Tri-Cities area of Washington State. Only the fae have "come out" when we start the series in *Moon Called.* Mercy is a former student of history but trained to work on German cars by the fae, Zee, a gremlin who, unlike most fae, can deal with iron. Mercy often works on Stefan's VW, a vampire who is obsessed with Scooby-Doo. The head of the local werewolf pack lives next to her and becomes a serious love interest. When a murdered werewolf ends up on her doorstep, things get nasty and filled with political intrigue. Whereas no one really figures out who Jane Yellowrock is, Mercy is more open and forthcoming and she has complex relationships with two werewolves and one vampire.

In *Blood Bound,* vampires have a more central role. Stefan, the vampire friend, asks Mercy for a favor, and she owes him. A demon has taken over a vampire and is raising chaos, creating havoc, and murdering randomly in the Tri-Cities. Mercy may be the only one who can bring the demon-vampire down. Although she is no match for most werewolves or vampires, walkers are somewhat immune to vampire magic and they also have the ability to talk to ghosts. There are scary meetings with the mistress of the vampire seethe, Marsilia, horrible encounters with the demon-possessed vampire, scenes of death and torture. Mercy Thompson doesn't start out as a vampire slayer, but she ends up as a slayer of rogue vampires, certain fae, and other monsters, because those she loves are in danger, hurt, or dying. The books provide a very different view of vampires than many on this list. Stefan is clearly deeply conflicted and trying to be a good guy, but this is a world where vampires need at least fourteen people (their menagerie) to feed on regularly if the people are not to die. Stefan is the only vampire who treats the humans who live with him with respect and keeps them healthy.

Book three, *Iron Kissed,* involves a series of murders on the fae reservation. Mercy gets in trouble with powerful fae who threaten to kill her as she learns more of the truth of fae life, which, for most humans, is hidden behind their glamour and when revealed is more sinister than it appears on the surface.

The fourth book, *Bone Crossed,* is my favorite so far because it concentrates on vampires and the complex relationship between Stefan and Mercy. Meanwhile Adam brings Mercy into the werewolf pack, which—since she is a coyote—is not welcomed by everyone. She begins to accept Adam's love and warmth. Suddenly, an emaciated, tortured, burnt Stefan appears—seemingly thrown out of the seethe and punished for allowing Mercy to kill a vampire. The next day, Mercy's shop is painted with graffiti, partly by the attacker's girlfriend, in anger over his death, but also by Marsilia—the head of the seethe—who paints a symbol of crossed bones, designating Mercy as a traitor to be killed. By the end of the novel we know that Marsilia has been playing a deep political game; she is using Stefan and Mercy to ferret out traitors to the seethe. Stefan, the only vampire who seems deeply moral in this series, is shown to be loyal and trustworthy.

Silver Borne, the fifth novel, has no vampires at all. Sam, her roommate, loses it and completely reverts to his wolf. He is in danger of being put down. Adam is challenged for pack Alpha, and resentments over Adam's love of Mercy are revealed. The fae involve Mercy in a complex plot.

Book six, *River Marked,* starts and ends with Stefan, who is emaciated, and only four of his people are left alive. Many were broken by Marsilia. The main element of the book takes place in a campground where Mercy and Adam have gone after their wedding. There is a river devil monster to defeat, and Mercy comes in contact with many Native American shifters, medicine people, and ancestors, including someone who might or might not be her father, and might even be something more.

The Kate Daniels series, by Ilona Andrews. Another post-*Buffy* slayer series is by Ilona Andrews and features Kate Daniels. The first book is *Magic Bites.* It takes place in a dystopian Atlanta where magic and technology vie with each other. Magic has destroyed most of the large buildings in Atlanta; cars stop running when magic is afoot; lights go out and are replaced by feylanterns. There are monsters galore, including two rival powers: the Pack, a group of shapeshifters led by the Beast Lord, also known as Curran, a feline shapeshifter; and the People, who seem to be necromancers who control vampires. The vampires here are totally bestial with no redeeming qualities; they are controlled by members of the People. Kate Daniels is a merc, a slayer, who is hired to take on some of these beasts when there are problems. She has a complex and almost fight-to-the-death relationship with Curran, the Beast Lord, and the various leaders of the People. She can use blood and fire to powerful effect, abilities she often keeps hidden. Kate is another one of these tough-talking women wearing worn jeans and rarely having a soft side. Her one attempt to have a date with a normal human doctor backfires miserably. The book is well written, and some of the descriptions are wonderful, but since I am concentrating on conflicted vampires and these vampires have no redeeming qualities, I will give the rest of the series a miss.

The Sonja Blue Collection, by Nancy A. Collins. Collins has written ten several Sonja Blue novels, which feature a badass vampire heroine who is also a slayer. The books are not particularly well written and the e-books have a startling number of mistakes and misprints. But Blue is a fierce and fascinating character, which kept me going through two novels. In *Sunglasses After Dark,* we learn that Blue was once a rich young woman brutally raped and left for dead by a powerful vampire. She survived, was turned, and became a renegade. Vampirism is an infection in this world, which is peopled by all kinds of supernatural beings: ogres, vargr (a kind of werewolf), demons, seraphim, and more. There are human sensitives who see the monsters and the Real World; most don't. Monsters are also called Pretenders. This is a very violent novel, dark and graphic with lots of blood and gore. But I kept it out of the horror section because Sonja is not evil, and she seems to be struggling to maintain some semblance of humanity despite vampire urges and the rage that consumes her and often leads her on killing sprees. There is also this demonic "Other" inside her which is never really spelled out. Vampires here have trouble in sunlight but can survive if they limit their time outside. They are not troubled by Christian symbols.

In the Blood, the second Sonja Blue novel, is better in many ways, since it involves a serious relationship between Blue and a human private investigator; there is even some intimacy between them. Blue wants to find her roots, and to kill Morgan, the vampire who raped her and left her for dead. Again, the errors in the e-books are distracting.

THE CLASSICS

Authors:

Sir Thomas Malory, Johann Wolfgang von Goethe, Robert Southey, Lord George Gordon Byron, Sir Walter Scott, John William Polidori, John Keats, Edgar Allan Poe, James Malcolm Rymer, Alexandre Dumas, Charles Pierre Baudelaire, Ivan Turgenev, William Gilbert, J. Sheridan Le Fanu, Eliza Lynn Linton, Julian Hawthorne, Sir Arthur Conan Doyle, Robert Louis Stevenson, Vasile Alecsandri, Anne Crawford, Guy de Maupassant, Mary Cholmondeley, Hume Nisbit, Ambrose Bierce, Mary Elizabeth Braddon, Bram Stoker, F. G. Loring

THIS SECTION INCLUDES poems, short stories, novellas, and novels that predate *Dracula*, as well as *Dracula, Carmilla,* and other vampire classics. I put them in chronological order because it will give you a sense of how much was written about vampires before *Dracula* and how many well-known poets and writers took to the subject. Looking at all these tales and poems at once, I was struck by how many were about men's fear of women's power.

Le Morte d'Arthur, **by Sir Thomas Malory.** This 1485 compilation of romantic tales includes one from 1470, which features a woman vampire. She needs the blood of royal virgins to survive.

"The Bride of Corinth," by Johann Wolfgang von Goethe. Written in 1797, this poem features probably the first female vampire who preys on a man. A man and a woman are pledged to each other; one is from a Christian family, one from a Pagan one. The young man is not told of the young woman's death. He arrives from Athens to Corinth, goes to bed, and is visited by his bride who has pale hands. We learn her lips are cold and she has no heartbeat. She kills him and says both of them should burn and they will go to their old gods.

"Thalaba, the Destroyer," by Robert Southey. There are many early poems featuring vampires. Robert Southey mentions vampires in his 1801 poem, "Thalaba, the Destroyer."

"The Giaour," by Lord Byron. Byron mentions vampires in his 1813 poem, "The Giaour": "But first on Earth as Vampyre sent, Thy corse shall from its tomb be rent. Then ghastly haunt the native place, And suck the blood of all thy race."

"Rokeby," by Sir Walter Scott. Sir Walter Scott has vampire verses in his 1813 poem "Rokeby."

"A Fragment of a Turkish Tale," by Lord Byron. In 1819, Lord Byron began but never finished a vampire story, "A Fragment of a Turkish Tale."

"The Vampyre," by John William Polidori. Published in 1819, "The Vampyre" is considered the first vampire short story in the English language. Polidori began to write at the Villa Diodati, near Lake Geneva, during the same rainy weekend in 1816 when Mary Shelley began *Frankenstein*. It was partly based on an unfinished Byron story. Polidori was Byron's physician. The story wanders all over the place and is poorly written; there are odd sections praising Byron, but it does pull together many elements from folklore and is regarded, along with *Carmilla,* as the work that most influenced Stoker and the modern vampire genre. Many novels, plays, and even operas are based on this tale. The story: Lord Ruthven aids the villainous and leads the innocent to ruin. An Englishman, Aubrey, notices that Ruthven is peculiar and travels with him. Aubrey meets a beautiful Greek girl, Ianthe, who tells Aubrey about vampires, which Aubrey discounts. Ianthe is killed by a vampire whom Aubrey later realizes is Lord Ruthven. Ruthven is wounded by robbers and dies but revives when he is placed in the moonlight. He later marries and kills Aubrey's sister. In this story you need to stake a vampire to kill it, and anyone who is bitten by a vampire will become a vampire.

"Lamia," by John Keats. This poem was published in 1819, the same year as Polidori's "The Vampyre." Lamia is a form of vampire. In the poem, Hermes, seeking a nymph, agrees to free the Lamia from her serpent form if she will reveal the nymph to him. The Lamia goes to Corinth where she has fallen for a youth named Lycius. All is set for the wedding, but one guest, the sophist, Apollonius, reveals the Lamia's true identity. She disappears, and the youth, Lycius, dies.

"Ligeia," by Edgar Allan Poe. First published in 1838, "Ligeia" is a weird short story. The first part just states the narrator's love for Ligeia, how she is perfect in form and brilliant in mind. This goes on for pages. When she sickens, she protests and fights against death, but she dies. The narrator marries again and creates a rich bed chamber for his new wife. She sickens and dies and revives many times, until he realizes it is his Ligeia returning as a vampire.

Varney the Vampire, or the Feast of Blood, **by James Malcolm Rymer.** This is a fascinating Victorian penny dreadful, eight hundred pages, and the writing veers from totally awful to lovely in small doses. It was serialized in 1845–47 and is a precursor to *Dracula.* Many of our ideas about vampires come from this work—Varney is pale, with long teeth, although he can go out in the sunlight and feeds only rarely. Vampires can revive if wounded by being under the light of the full moon. At first Varney is an object of horror who feasts on a young woman, Flora Bannerworth, but Varney turns out to be fairly moral; he does not want to kill anyone; he attacks Flora only because he wants money. Varney may well be the first morally conflicted vampire we see in literature. Most scholars attribute this book to James Malcolm Rymer, although others maintain it is by Thomas Preskett Prest.

When I started this book, I thought it was awful, but as the book proceeds, it gets more interesting. There are good insights about the behavior of mobs. Varney and other suspected vampires are hunted down, and the description of the character of small towns and townspeople who forsake their reason is quite brilliant.

There are also good comic characters like Jack Pringle, the seaman, and there are interludes—tales about knights and about life on the sea. There are several versions and the one I read, all 812 pages, did not have certain parts that are described by scholars. In one version, Varney commits suicide in Italy, which did not get a mention in the edition I read.

"The Vampire of the Carpathian Mountains," by Alexandre Dumas. Published in 1849 as part of *A Thousand and One Ghosts,* this is a fascinating story of a woman who escapes the Russians and tries to find a monastery in the Carpathians, but she is stopped by brigands and then rescued by the brother of the chief brigand. The horrible brother who lusts for the woman has no shadow and no reflection. After his death, he preys on her; she is rescued, but there is tragedy. A long-time curse on the family is finally broken. Vampires in this story are pale, killed by stakes, and have no reflection, but sunlight is not a problem.

"Les Fleurs du Mal," by Charles Pierre Baudelaire. Baudelaire wrote a poem about a vampire woman; the poem was one of six taken from *Les Fleurs du Mal,* which was published in 1857.

"Phantoms," by Ivan Turgenev. In 1864, the Russian writer Ivan Turgenev wrote the short story "Phantoms," which describes a (probable) vampire woman who takes the protagonist flying all through Europe and even into the past, into Roman times; it's not exactly clear what she is.

"The Last Lords of Gardonal," by William Gilbert. This story was published in 1867. A baron of cruel temperament, who has tormented those on his lands, finds a beautiful farmer's daughter. She refuses him, as does her father. The baron punishes the family by setting fire to the house and doesn't realize the daughter has been killed in the fire. A learned astrologer sends a message that he will give the baron information about the girl and bring her to him, after he frees some hostages. The bride appears, totally beautiful; the wedding takes place, but later, as the baron kisses the bride, she turns into a corpse and sucks his blood, until he is weak. He escapes. She follows and offers him blood, which he refuses, although she says it will restore him. Night comes. She sucks from him again and he dies.

Carmilla, **by J. Sheridan Le Fanu.** This novella, about one hundred pages long, was written in 1872. It predates Bram Stoker's *Dracula* by twenty-five years and influenced Stoker and many vampire novelists who followed. Several movies have been made about Carmilla, and she is described in Kim Newman's Anno Dracula books as a friend of Geneviève. The story is compelling and easy to read in one sitting. It's very gothic and I personally think the writing is better than Stoker's *Dracula.* It is the story of a young girl, Laura, who lives a lonely life and has just learned that one of her best friends has died. Suddenly a carriage appears with a mother and daughter. The daughter, Carmilla, comes to stay with much mystery about it. Carmilla is utterly beautiful and the attachment between her and Laura is strong; there is some subtle lesbian eroticism. Slowly, Laura finds herself beset by dreams; she feels a sudden pain in her breast. Carmilla locks herself in her tomb and doesn't rise until late afternoon. Laura's father finds a picture of the Countess Millarca from the 1600s, and it is clearly Carmilla. Vampires in this tale can walk in the sun; they seem to be able to go through walls and have other powers. Staking and beheading are the only ways to kill them. On the surface Carmilla is beautiful and sweet, but she is cunning inside. It is a tale filled with gothic atmospherics, but there are loose ends. For example, where is the mother who left her daughter off, feigning an emergency? Who and what was she?

"The Fate of Madame Cabanel," by Eliza Lynn Linton. Published in 1880, this is a very simple story of vigilantism. A French rural town is filled with superstitious people. The only learned person, Jules Cabanel, is the mayor and the justice of the peace. He goes to England and takes an English wife. She is young, healthy looking, and immediately arouses suspicion. Also, she takes walks in a graveyard and doesn't know her Catholic prayers well—probably because she is a Protestant. When people get sick and she remains red lipped and healthy, rumors abound that she is a vampire. When a child dies, the townspeople grab her and kill her. Jules Cabanel metes out punishments.

"Ken's Mystery," by Julian Hawthorne. Published in 1884, this interesting story is by the son of Nathaniel Hawthorne. The narrator has a formerly outgoing friend, Ken, who went to Europe and came back very much changed. Ken brings out the banjo the narrator gave him a while back, but it is now rotted and seems several hundred years old. Ken tells him the story of going to Ireland and meeting a woman by a graveyard on All Hallows' Eve. He comes back to the town, finds a great building, and the lady invites him in. All is beautiful but cold, both her and the fireplace. She doesn't kill him or seem to suck his blood; she seems more like an energy vampire. He wakes up weak but alive. The house and the banjo are in ruins.

"John Barrington Cowles," by Sir Arthur Conan Doyle. Published in 1884, three years before the first Sherlock Holmes stories, this is the tale of an extraordinary woman with great beauty and powers of mind, clearly a mind vampire, but also with the seeming ability to turn into a wolf. Much of Kate Northcott's powers are left mysterious, but she is engaged to three men, and all die, presumably after they learn the truth about this woman. They run from her; she calls them back to her, and to their death. The writing is lovely.

"Olalla," by Robert Louis Stevenson. This short story was published in 1885. A military man recovering from his wounds in Spain seeks mountain air by going to live with a formerly well-established and once noble but now impoverished family. The son speaks and sings oddly and has little intellect and at one point devours a squirrel raw in the forest. The mother just sits in the sunlight but greets him every day. A storm comes, a black wind, and he finds himself locked in his room and hears screams in the night. Later, he searches the house, finds a room with old books and a recently written poem expressing grief and sadness. He realizes this must be the daughter, Olalla, whom he meets, finds beautiful, and determines to marry. She tells him he must leave. He cuts his hand and goes to the slumbering mother for help. Suddenly, she bites him to the bone and he is pulled off by the son. He hears the screams again. Olalla meets him and tells him to go. He does. In a last meeting, she compares her sacrifices with those of Christ. In some of the discussions of this story, there is the notion that the family has lost intellect and refinement through inbreeding, a theme in some gothic fiction. The mother is attempting to get purer blood.

"The Vampire," by Vasile Alecsandri. Alecsandri was a Romanian nationalist, called by some the Victor Hugo of Eastern Europe. This lovely poem was published in 1886. A vampire rises in the night, but the knight who doesn't heed his love's warning is dashed to the ground, dead along with his horse.

"A Mystery of the Campagna," by Anne Crawford. In this 1887 tale, two different men tell the story of Marcello who finds a place in the Italian Campagna to write music and falls under the sway of a female vampire from Roman times who leads him down to a sepulcher and sucks him dry.

"The Horla," by Guy de Maupassant. In this short story, published in 1887, A man sees a Brazilian three-masted ship on the Seine, and ever after he is haunted by a mysterious being. He suddenly feels ill every night. He notes that water and milk disappear. The being comes to dominate his thoughts. He feels he is going insane. The narration is in the form of a journal and there are a lot of philosophical musings, even the possibility of this being an alien species that will take over the Earth. In the end, he sets fire to his house, but that doesn't end the problem.

"Let Loose," by Mary Cholmondeley. This is a strange but effective story, published in 1890. A man is asked why he wears such high collars. He tells the story of looking for a fresco his father painted in the crypt of a church in Yorkshire. He finds the church but is told that the crypt has been locked for years; something bad happened there. He persuades the clergyman to give him the keys; he finds the fresco and starts working on it over three days. On each of the first two days, someone dies; on the last day, his dog goes mad and attacks him, but the scars are not those of a dog, which is why he wears those collars.

"The Old Portrait" and "The Vampire Maid," by Hume Nisbet. In "The Old Portrait," published in 1890, a man buys a picture frame, washes away the painting within, only to find another painting underneath of a beautiful, pale woman. He notices the frame has snakes and skulls. It is a vampire painting, and she comes out, kisses him, intoxicates him, and starts to drain and possess him. He gets weaker and she gets stronger until, near death, he pushes her off, notices that she is more ripe and lifelike; he slashes the painting and burns it.

In Nisbet's "The Vampire Maid," also published in 1890, a man takes a cottage on the moor by the ocean, miles from anyone. There is a housekeeper and her sick daughter. He falls in love but every night has disturbing dreams. Again, he gets weaker and she gets stronger. Then one night, he suddenly awakens; she comes as a bat and bites his arm and he sees the bodies of many young men who have died. He escapes.

"The Death of Halpin Frayser," by Ambrose Bierce. In this short story. published in 1893, Frayser is a Southerner who is the descendant of a well-known poet, but he has little talent. He travels to California where he dreams of a forest of blood and being strangled. When investigators find him dead, they find a half-written poem that he has written in blood in the "dream." It's as good as the work of his more talented ancestor.

"Good Lady Ducayne," by Mary Elizabeth Braddon. Published in 1896, "Good Lady Ducayne" tells the story of Bella Rolleston, who takes a position as a rich lady's companion in order to help her mother who is poor. Several companions before her have died. She travels with her employer to Italy and starts feeling ill. She has weird dreams. It turns out she is being bled and given chloroform so that the doctor can give her blood to the old woman, believing it will keep her young.

Dracula, **by Bram Stoker.** Most people know this story, so this is a very short synopsis. Jonathan Harker, a young English lawyer, travels to Castle Dracula in Transylvania to conclude a real estate deal. He is warned by villagers; he is attacked by wolves. Harker is welcomed, but eventually made a prisoner by Dracula; he is attacked by three female vampires and finally barely escapes. Meanwhile, near the town of Whitby, in England, a Russian ship is wrecked, its crew and captain dead. The cargo is fifty boxes of earth from Castle Dracula. Lucy Westenra, a friend of Harker's fiancée, Mina, begins to sleepwalk and is clearly being turned by the Count. Dr. Seward and his mentor, Van Helsing, put garlic around Lucy's room. They also give her transfusions, which don't work. Lucy dies; she is eventually staked and laid to rest. The rest of the story concerns saving Mina, forcing Dracula back to Transylvania, and finally killing him. And of course there is crazy Renfield eating flies and all the other fun stuff.

It's quite a gothic slog, but much of the current view we have of vampires comes from this 1897 novel. It wasn't the first or even the second in the English language, but it has staying power. Many of our ideas about vampires, such as the idea that you can't see a vampire in a mirror, or that you have to invite a vampire in, come from this novel. Interestingly, the idea of vampires being averse to sunlight does not originate in Stoker's *Dracula*; we owe that idea to later films. Dracula could function during the day; he was just weaker. A very interesting analysis of the Christian elements in *Dracula* can be found in *The Vampire Defanged,* by Susannah Clements (2011).

ANNE RICE CLASSICS

The Vampire Chronicles:

Interview with the Vampire, The Vampire Lestat, The Queen of the Damned, The Tale of the Body Thief, Memnoch the Devil, The Vampire Armand, Merrick, and *Blood and Gold*

RICE HAS SOLD MORE than seventy-five million books. Some of the writing in these novels is powerful, and the characters stay with you.

Interview with the Vampire. Anne Rice wrote *Interview with the Vampire* in 1976. It started as a short story and was expanded after her daughter died of leukemia. This is the story of Louis, clearly one of the first morally struggling, reluctant, and conflicted vampires. I go in and out of liking the sultry, gothic, Anne Rice world of New Orleans, but this is clearly the book that took the genre in a very different direction. Louis tells his story to Daniel Molloy, a mortal journalist who figures in later books when he is turned himself. This is the story of Louis and Lestat, the making of the child vampire, Claudia, the meeting of Armand and other vampires in Paris. It is the story of Louis and his reluctance to kill. Claudia kills easily and hates her condition; she almost kills Lestat, by poisoning him and leaving him in a swamp. She is finally killed by Armand and those in the Théatre des Vampires in Paris. By the end of the book, Louis is alone and telling his story to Daniel.

The Vampire Lestat. This 1985 novel takes Lestat from his boyhood in pre-revolutionary France to his escape from his family and his move to Paris. He meets Magnus, a rogue vampire who turns him. Lestat turns his friend Nicolas—a bad move—and he turns his own mother, Gabrielle, who darts in and out of the various books, preferring to be alone and in nature. There are complicated scenes with Armand, bringing vampires out of darkness into the Théatre des Vampires. Later he meets Marius, a two-thousand-year-old vampire who is guarding Akasha and Enkil, Those Who Must Be Kept. They are the first vampires, whose history you learn in the subsequent book, *The Queen of the Damned.* Against the wishes of Marius, Lestat awakens them from their seeming unconscious state. Akasha and Lestat share blood, which makes Lestat extremely strong. Enkil tries to kill Lestat, but he is saved by Marius. The novel ends in modern times with Lestat writing the book and becoming a rock star. The first half is utterly gripping, and as with much of Rice's work, the writing is detailed and flowery. I list this title among my favorites in "The Best" section.

The Queen of the Damned. This complicated novel, published in 1988, puts forth the origin of all vampires according to Rice, which goes back to the land of Kemet, which later becomes Egypt. The king and queen, Akasha and Enkil, want power over two witches,

Mekare and Maharet, who live in another land. The fight is really between those who believe in eating the dead ritually versus those who believe in mummification. An evil spirit turns Akasha into the first vampire and there is a sense that she holds the thread—that if anything happens to her, all vampires will die. So that is why Marius is keeping Those Who Must Be Kept so safely. The queen gets loose and wants to create a society without violence; she aims to do that by killing ninety-nine out of each hundred men. Vampires start dying; Lestat is repelled by her vision but also becomes her lover. A small group of vampires is saved, including Maharet, Marius, Pandora, Santino, Mael, Khayman, Amand, Eric, Gabrielle, Daniel, Louis, and the newest vampire, Jesse, who is a relative of Maharet. The climax of the book comes when Mekare, in anger, kills the queen and becomes the new Queen of the Damned. Some parts of the book are fabulous, some quite disjointed.

The Tale of the Body Thief. A much simpler story, *The Tale of the Body Thief* (1992) involves Lestat, who continues to be impossible, an impulsive prankster who leaps first and then looks. He is tired, tries to kill himself in the sun, but he is too strong. He realizes he is alone and begins to develop his relationship with the human David Talbot, who is a member of the Talamasca, an order that keeps watch over occult happenings. David and Lestat end up having a complicated but deep friendship. Meanwhile a strange man appears, Raglan James, who tells Lestat that he knows how to trade bodies. He knows Lestat wants to experience being human again. The plan is to do it for a short time, but there are warnings that James is a liar and a thief. Lestat, being impulsive, does it, even though everyone tells him this is a dangerous and foolish move. He ends up in a young, gorgeous body, and Raglan James becomes a vampire with some of Lestat's strengths, although he is clumsy. Lestat hates being human; he gets cold, his eyesight is so bad that he often feels almost blind or in a mist; he is hurt easily. Eating is not so pleasant; pissing and bowel movements are even worse. The only true wonder is the sun. Lestat also gets to have normal sex, which the vampires in Rice's world are unable to experience.

Memnoch the Devil. The next book in the Vampire Chronicles, *Memnoch the Devil* (1995), is one of Rice's most intense and ambitious books—it was not an easy read. It is told in the voice of Lestat, who is following a corrupt criminal with a huge collection of ancient, mostly religious, artifacts, including books by Wynken, an author, artist, and medieval heretic. The criminal has a beautiful daughter, Dora, who is a kind of religious guru. When the criminal is killed he comes back as a ghost and convinces Lestat to protect Dora and take the artifacts. Meanwhile, Lestat realizes he is being stalked by a powerful being that is clearly a Satan figure. The heart of the book is an intense journey where Lestat meets the angel Memnoch and God, and much of it is Memnoch's retelling of the battle between God and Satan in a new way in which Memnoch is pleading for human souls to have a road to heaven. Memnoch wants Lestat to be his deputy. The book retells the entire creation of the world by God, who sees humans as a mere part of nature and doesn't really care about their suffering. Memnoch shows Lestat the suffering due to wars done in religion's name; he experiences the Crusades, the burning of Jews, and the death of witches. He actually sees Christ on the cross and tastes his blood. Memnoch's critique of God is that he doesn't truly understand human suffering and that it is love, sexual union, and the creation of tribes and families that brings humans to a place above nature and close to the heavenly beings. Memnoch does bring many souls to heaven and is later given the task of bringing more. At the end, Lestat rejects the task he has been given by Memnoch and returns to Earth with the veil of Veronica, which Dora uses to proclaim miracles on Earth. It's a fascinating book. It's easy to see how obsessed Rice has always been with Christianity.

The Vampire Armand. It took me a couple of months to get through *The Vampire Armand* (1998). This is Armand's tale told to David Talbot. We hear the story of Armand's beginning in Eastern Europe, near Kiev in the 15th century. He has a mother who designs painted eggs, and he is taken into a monastery where he becomes a painter of icons. But later he is captured and sold to work in a brothel. He is bought by Marius and taken to Venice. He lives a rich life, filled with art and painting, and is taken under Marius's wing. They become lovers of a sort, and he is educated. Marius slowly reveals his vampire nature to Armand. When Armand is wounded by an enemy, Marius turns him. But eventually his world comes crashing down when a group of vampires led by Santino seemingly kill Marius, imprison Armand and insist he join their odd, very Christian, vampire cult. They see themselves as the children of darkness, not allowed to traffic in the ways of man, wear colors, consort with humans, or go into churches. Armand becomes part of this cult. He takes over the Paris Coven that eventually becomes the Théatre des Vampires. After almost killing himself by embracing the sun, he comes upon two children, a mad player of Beethoven and a Bedouin youth who takes care of her. Against Armand's wishes, Marius makes the two youngsters vampires. At the end of the book Armand talks about the tragedy of "all of us, those who kill to live and thrive on death, even as the very earth decrees it, and are cursed with consciousness to know it." Later Marius, after turning the young people into vampires, says he is no longer optimistic about the world's improvement. He once was a rationalist, but now he believes only love can make us forget all savagery.

Merrick. *Merrick* (2000) is a very nicely structured novel, simple and quite riveting. It brings together the Vampire Chronicles and the Lives of the Mayfair Witches series, also by Anne Rice. David Talbot, the former Talamasca superior, now a vampire, is asked by Louis to convince Merrick to do a spell that would allow Louis to speak to the ghost of Claudia and determine if she is at rest. We learn the story of Merrick, a very powerful witch who is given to the Talamasca by her relative, another powerful witch, the Great Nananne. David, who once loved Merrick when he was an elderly man, before he changed bodies and became a vampire, comes to see her. She is drunk, which is not unusual, but she agrees to contact Claudia. When she meets Louis she is smitten with him and he is smitten with her, to David's own pain. They do the spell, and Claudia appears but says she is not at rest. She says she has such hatred for Louis, she hopes he will kill himself and experience the same nothingness that she knows. Merrick is convinced the spirit has lied and is simply feeding on Louis's fears; Louis, who is about to do himself in, is suddenly so taken with Merrick that all he wants is to be with her. David fears that Louis will destroy her mortality—a not unreasonable fear. Then Louis lies out in the sun, becoming a blackened and lifeless body, but he revives with the blood of Lestat, David, and Merrick, and becomes strong. David, Louis, Lestat, and Merrick become a new coven together. The Talamasca orders them to leave New Orleans and regards them as enemies. The four vampires leave no trace and disappear. The most interesting theological idea in the book is that there really is nothing out there, despite previous novels where Lestat meets Jesus and the devil and experiences heaven and hell.

Blood and Gold. *Blood and Gold* (2001) is the life story of Marius. He is abducted by Druids, who see him as a replacement for their god of the grove, but he escapes, not wanting to spend his life in a tree. He goes to Egypt, ends up becoming the guardians of Those Who Must Be Kept, falls in love with a mortal woman, Pandora, and turns her. Later, in the Renaissance, he becomes a painter and the protector of Armand. This book also gives another version of the meeting with Lestat, of Lestat's drinking of the blood of Akasha, and the destruction of Akasha by Mekare.

Anne Rice continues this series with *Blackwood Farm* (2002) and *Blood Canticle* (2003). Her vampire saga goes on in the New Tales of the Vampires series, which includes *Pandora* (1998) and *Vittorio the Vampire* (1999).

NOVELS in the CLASSIC TRADITION

Authors:

Fred Saberhagen, Tim Powers, Elizabeth Kostova,
Carlos Fuentes, B. E. Scully, Lucius Shepard

THESE ARE MODERN AUTHORS who write gothic-type novels. Also I am including some reimaginings of *Dracula*.

The Dracula Sequence, by Fred Saberhagen. *The Dracula Tape* is the first of a series of books in which Saberhagen re-visions Dracula as a good guy, and Dr. Van Helsing as the one who killed Lucy and almost killed Mina through medical ignorance. After all, this was before blood types were known, and Lucy is given blood transfusions. Dracula is not affected by Catholic symbols and is a practicing Catholic. The book takes place in the 1970s; Dracula still exists and puts his version of the story on tape for the descendants of Jonathan and Mina Harker. Dracula gives some alternate explanations for what Stoker wrote about, and some of them are quite convincing. There are some similarities here with *Dracula in Love*, by Karen Essex, a more recent feminist re-visioning of the Dracula myth (see Adult Romance).

An Old Friend of the Family is my favorite, so far, of this moral Dracula series by Saberhagen. In this book Dracula's vampire enemies attempt to take him down by preying on a wealthy family, the Southerlands, who happen to be descendants of Mina Harker. Kate Southerland is kidnapped by evil vampires, turned, and strangely un-turned at the end, seemingly through an intense stress reaction. Another child is kidnapped and seriously injured. A third Southerland, Judy, finds herself in a strange alliance with Dracula, who is never called by that name, but who takes the name of a French doctor, Corday. Twice, the evil vampires call him Vlad Tepes, so it becomes clear. There are references to people speaking in a language like Latin, which is clearly a veiled reference to Romania. Judy and others help Corday, never exactly knowing who or what he is, although some find out by the book's end. There are murders and kidnappings, and the story is quite gripping and well paced. The writing is quite good, although there are a surprising number of typos and misspellings throughout. As with the original Dracula, vampires are stronger at night and are able to turn into mist and animals; they don't reflect in mirrors and have to be invited in. But Dracula is not super strong; he actually needs some human help, which makes the book more interesting.

The Stress of Her Regard, by Tim Powers. Oh, what a totally irritating book, although it's gotten all kinds of fabulous reviews. It oozes with the gothic and romantic, but it's very disjointed, and at page 200, I almost gave up. It takes place during the time of Byron, Keats, Shelley, and the romantic poets. The atmosphere is gothic fog. Our protagonist, Michael Crawford, has suffered the death of his brother and first wife; while drunk, on the night before his wedding, he puts the ring of his wife-to-be on a statue. He finds the fist of the statue closed when he searches, and the next thing he knows, his wife is murdered in their bed on their wedding night and he must flee for his life, accused of the murder. He changes his name and tries to flee from the succubus, lamia, or whatever vampiric female thing is chasing him, part serpent and part ethereal woman. He meets up with the three Romantic poets who are also being chased by similar beings. The beings mark them somehow and those that are marked recognize each other. Sometimes they lose a finger as a sign; some are prey and die; but others are part of the family, like Crawford is through marriage, and Shelley is through birth. Those who have been infected are often pale and sickly looking. There are words used to describe them that I can't find in any dictionary, like "neffer." Mary Shelley is portrayed as if all her ideas came from her husband, and she is a cipher; in fact, only the men seem mildly interesting, and none of the characters are really developed. Polidori has a role as Byron's doctor, whom Crawford replaces, but there is nary a mention of his story "The Vampyre." There are sphinxes, rock monsters, muses, and creatures from Greek myth. Some of the writing is beautiful, particularly in the last third, and the entire story has an eerie feel. But it is all too gloomy for me.

The Historian, **by Elizabeth Kostova.** It took me months to get into this book. It is more than six hundred pages long. I started it twice and finally got absorbed. There are parts that are compelling and suspenseful; other parts are too much like a travelogue through Eastern Europe. There is a lot of history of the Ottoman Empire, the war between Christians and Turks, and the history of Vlad Tepes and his cruelty. We follow a number of different people through their travels and letters—a young girl and her father, the woman her father loves, and a professor who has disappeared. And all this takes place while traipsing through much of Eastern Europe during the Soviet period. But the central idea is that Dracula, Vlad Tepes, is still alive and wreaking evil. He has placed a book with blank pages and his dragon symbol in the path of different scholars who then try to find the truth, while Dracula tries to ensnare them, searching for a historian to organize his library. Some of the writing is lovely and some of the characters, like the protagonist, Helen, are compelling. It's all a bit weird, if somewhat fascinating.

***Vlad,* by Carlos Fuentes.** This novella is a very odd retelling of the Dracula story. There is too much tumult in Eastern Europe, so Vlad Tepes comes to Mexico, a perfect place to disappear into the multitudes and prey on people. The protagonist, Yves Navarro, works for a strange and unemotional lawyer, Don Eloy Zurinaga. Zurinaga asks Navarro to help him procure a house for a friend, a count from the Balkans. Guess who? Navarro's wife is a realtor and helps him find the house—one with drains and no windows. It then goes to form with coffins and dirt and even the Bela Lugosi line about drinking wine. Navarro's wife becomes attracted to Dracula, and Dracula seeks the couple's daughter as a playmate for his ten-year-old vampire daughter. It's all fairly predictable. The wife, Asuncion, finds sex with Dracula enjoyable and, after all, her child will become immortal. The end is horrific, mysterious, and a bit unclear. This is a very short book, 120 pages, and there are some good meditations on mortality.

Verland: The Transformation, **by B. E. Scully.** This is a compelling book and deeper than it first appears. Elle Bramasol writes true crime novels. She has known tragedy and death, including her mother's murder. She is assigned to do a book on a Hollywood mogul, now in jail for murder. When she meets the man, Kingman, he is not interested in his guilt or innocence but leads her to read a diary of a vampire who tells of his one-hundred-year journey. Kingman wants to find him to gain immortality. The journal is beautiful, with hints of Anne Rice. Verland, the vampire, describes the horror of his transformation, his life through various wars, his need to kill, and his experiments with abstaining. He has periods of isolation and other times when he lives in cities and mingles with people and other vampires and involves himself in the arts. The book is filled with philosophical musings on death, the afterlife, and the joys and tragedies of immortality. The writing is excellent and the questions posed are serious. What starts out as a simple true crime investigation ends up asking large questions about the value of human life.

The Golden, **by Lucius Shepard.** An odd and erotic novel; vampires have gathered in the strange and huge castle Banat that is out of a fantasy—endless rooms filled with grotesque things, people in each of them. These vampires have gathered in the castle for a special event three hundred years in the making—the decanting. A young girl has been bred over generations to have the most sublime blood. Before this event can happen, she is murdered, and Michael Beheim, a new member of the family, only a vampire for several years, is put in charge of the investigation. Vampires, in Shepard's world, are superbly strong and are made through a process called judgment, where they are brought close to death, and most do not survive. They live in the dark, though this book supposes that a secret potion has been discovered that allows them to be in the daylight, since the murder occurs during the day. The vampires feed off humans, many of whom attach themselves to the family in the hopes that, despite the risks, they will have a chance for judgment. Vampires also undergo a final death in which revelations take place and truths are discovered. Political warfare among branches of the family is constant; sex and love take second place to political intrigue and debauchery. The writing is a bit flowery and turgid for my taste, but the novel explores evil and good. Take this wonderful passage spoken by the Patriarch, the vampire leader in the book:

> Those devoted to the good perceive themselves and everyone like them to be intrinsically imperfect; they seek to impose order on their lives, to limit the natural urges. . . . And what has been the result of their efforts? War. Famine. Torture. Rape. The slaughter and incarceration of millions. . . . Moreover those of us who favor evil, profess ourselves to be natural creatures and strive only to express our natures. We feed when we must, we give way to rage and lust . . . we deny ourselves nothing, and we accept the truth of who and what we are. . . . Some die at our hands. . . . On occasion we overindulge, but never on such grand and fulminate scale as the overindulgences of the Christians. . . . They have no understanding of moderation.

UNIQUE, ODD, and UNCLASSIFIABLE VAMPIRE NOVELS

Authors:

Theodore Sturgeon, S. L. Juers, Tananarive Due, Wayne Josephson, Janice Eidus, Steven Van Patten, Steven Brust, Kathryn Leigh Scott

Some of Your Blood, **by Theodore Sturgeon.** Sturgeon is a well-known science fiction writer, yet this short novel, really almost a novella, is not science fiction. It's a dark and rather beautiful story of a much damaged man, George, who starts drinking blood at an early age, when his mother's breasts bleed. He hunts, drinks blood of animals, and has a girlfriend, although there is almost no sex. The story is told partly from his journal—as he is someone who can write, but doesn't talk much—and partly by the psychiatrists who are trying to figure out who he is and fill in his history. George cares for people, but he is also a killer. He is free from his obsession at certain times—when he is in the army and when he is in jail. He does drink blood from his girlfriend, Anna. George hits an officer and is placed in a mental institution; after that, there is a long saga of learning through psychological tests what really makes him tick. One mysterious line in a letter to his girlfriend, Anna, makes it clear that things are not quite what they seem. The last twenty pages are stark, horrible but beautiful. This is more of a psychological thriller than a straight horror story or vampire tale, but there is something deeply sweet about the caring and yet murderous character of George.

***Eternally Yours,* by S. L. Juers.** I am guessing this is self-published. It is a journal of a man who was made a vampire at the time of the American Revolution and charts his life until the present. Good idea, but the writing is flawed.

***My Soul to Keep,* by Tananarive Due.** A very unusual novel by an African American writer. A woman journalist, Jessica, marries and has a child by an immortal, although she is not aware of what he is. David, whose real name is Dawit, and who has lived since the 16th century, is not a vampire in the sense of needing blood, but he was created as an immortal by receiving blood during a ritual. Jessica is a journalist; David is a professor. But he is being called back by others who are part of a secret group of long-lived people. His attempt to keep the secret from his wife, stay with his wife and child, and escape the group that is coming for him leads him to do immoral actions, some with deeply troubling aspects. The ending is unexpected and somewhat unsatisfying, but it is a gripping and captivating book.

***Emma and the Vampires,* by Wayne Josephson.** We might as well say something about these mashups, from *Pride and Prejudice and Zombies* to this book, to *Mr. Darcy, Vampyre,* to *Dick and Jane and Vampires.* I haven't read *Mr. Darcy,* but *Emma* is just plain horrible, and I couldn't get through *Pride and Prejudice and Zombies* completely, although the scenes of the women fighting zombies in their long skirts provided a moment, but only a moment, of hilarity. But there is nothing here except a gimmick and a joke that lasts for about five minutes. I am amazed that these books have had such traction. There is no soul, passion, or story, and they certainly don't have the lovely sensibility of real Austen or Brontë novels, nor do they achieve any of the things that make vampire novels attractive: the explorations of mortality, power, identity, romance, and more. If you are desperate to look at one, take one out of the library, or spend five minutes skimming the pages at your local bookstore.

***The Last Jewish Virgin: A Novel of Fate,* by Janice Eidus.** This is a very fresh and different take on the vampire myth, and you don't really know until the end of the book whether we are talking real or fantasy. Lilith Zaremba is starting art school in lower Manhattan. Her mother is a feminist activist and writer. Zaremba meets Baron Rock, an art teacher who looks most vampiric. She, herself, dresses in a Goth manner and sits for him while he paints her portrait. Her mother also finds him compelling. Meanwhile, she befriends another art student, Colin, who seems blessedly normal. She is a virgin and extremely concerned with who is Jewish and who is not. She understands vampires as "a metaphor for repressed desire. For artistic creation. For madness. For the outcast inside us all. For the monster inside us all; it's about bestowing death and granting life, about being both savior and destroyer." It's a very short book, less than 150 pages, but a rather unique mix of Jewish, New York, feminist, and vampire—definitely different.

Brookwater's Curse Vol. I, by Steven Van Patten. This is a very unusual book. It looks self-published, by someone with a foot in the film, art, and anime world. It is the story of an African American vampire seen through his journals, and it details slavery, the Civil War, Reconstruction, all the way up to modern times. There are wonderful details about the horrors of slavery, about W. E. B. Du Bois, the KKK, and the Black Panthers. Quite a bit of the book takes place in Japan and Senegal. Christian Brookwater becomes a vampire and later a constable who aids the World Vampire Council in the fight against werewolves. There is a long section where he trains to be a vampire samurai in Japan. He falls in love, has a kid, and loses many who are dear to him. At the end he is imprisoned by the council because he has killed his mentor Caramano—although we don't know by the end of volume I whether this murder is justified. The novel is better on history than on character development. I have not read volume II.

Agyar, by Steven Brust. This is a very original but unsatisfying novel, and like many unsatisfying vampire novels, it is written in the first person by a man talking about his life. The writing is uneven, but very spare. There is no mention of the word "vampire" in the whole book—which is one of its charms. And yet, in the end, you know that is what Agyar is; there is no mention of feeding off the blood of others, though it clearly happens throughout the novel. Agyar Janus, or Jack Agyar, as he calls himself, is living in the town of Lakota, Ohio. He drinks only coffee, and later you learn that food sickens him. There is no mention of problems with sunlight until near the end, but if you pick up the clues, he needs to be invited in and he sleeps in the ground. Jack Agyar is living as a human, associating with university types, but he is dominated and controlled by a woman named Laura, who is clearly his maker and who decides to destroy him in a plot to implicate him for the people she has killed. He attempts to fight back. He feeds on prostitutes and on the human women he meets, but he usually allows them to live. He lives in a haunted, abandoned house and his main confidant is an African American ghost named Jim. He spends most of his time typing this story on an old typewriter. He also writes poems. His life is as boring as any normal human's. Clearly, this is a book where immortality can be a curse, and Agyar's only respite is trying to live and be with humans. He is harsh, amoral, not very nice, yet occasionally tender. It's all terribly sad and lugubrious.

***Dark Passages,* by Kathryn Leigh Scott.** You might think that a book written by a former actor in *Dark Shadows* might be interesting. You would be wrong. The book involves a vampire named Meg Harrison who gets a part in a show called *Dark Passages*. It takes place during the Cold War and the Kennedy Era, around the time of JFK's death. Meg is a secret vampire, brought up by a vampire mother who teaches her to resist blood. She drinks blood only from small animals when she needs to, and so she is not really at the height of her powers. No one on the show knows what she is, except one other actor, a woman named Camilla, who is a three-hundred-year-old powerful witch with a grudge against Meg's family. The witch kills someone Meg loves. This forces Meg to drink more and become more powerful. The book doesn't work because

Meg, who changes her name for the theater to Morgana, doesn't reveal herself to anyone. There is a real absence of passion or tension. Interestingly, the actor who plays the vampire in the show tells Meg *his* secrets, that he comes from a communist family, but she never reveals anything about herself. It's a rather lackluster effort.

LESBIAN VAMPIRE FICTION

Authors:

J. Sheridan Le Fanu (*see* The Classics), Pam Keesey,
Jewelle Gomez, Gary Bowen, Carol Leonard, Lawrence Schimel

SOME HAVE SAID that Elizabeth Bathory, who lived in the 17th century and bathed in the blood of her female victims, was a lesbian, but there is no evidence. There have been many films with overt use of vampires as lesbians, including *The Hunger, Mark of Lilith,* and *Because the Dawn.* The two books I read are anthologies and both are edited by Pam Keesey.

Daughters of Darkness: Lesbian Vampire Stories, **edited by Pam Keesey.** In this 1993 collection, there is a long introduction about vampires and their association with goddesses, the power of birth, death, and renewal, as well as all that was considered evil in Christianity, all that is dangerous and sexual. Lilith and Eve are both associated with the social and sexual improprieties of women. The introduction mentions Coleridge's Geraldine and Elizabeth Bathory, and a central part of the anthology is J. Sheridan Le Fanu's *Carmilla.* Keesey writes that Elizabeth Bathory and *Carmilla* inspired a golden age of lesbian vampire movies in the 1970s. The stories, besides *Carmilla*, are all over the map. She includes writers well-known in the lesbian community such as a selection from *The Gilda Stories* by Jewelle Gomez, "Louisiana: 1850." This is the lovely tale of a young escaped slave who is rescued by a three-hundred-year-old vampire who owns a brothel. The story is about the girl's coming of age, the choices she makes, and those that are forced on her as the Civil War approaches.

Dark Angels: Lesbian Vampire Stories, edited by Pam Keesey. In this 1995 anthology, Keesey describes the difference between *Daughters of Darkness* and *Dark Angels* this way: the first is a collection of lesbian fiction featuring vampires and vampire-related themes—stories of lesbian romance, coming out, stories deeply rooted in the women's movement and lesbian and gay civil rights. She describes *Dark Angels* as a collection of vampire stories featuring lesbians and lesbian-related themes. She writes that blood and the moon are associated with both vampires and the Goddess. Among the stories, "Blood Wedding" by Gary Bowen is a lovely tale about a 19th-century formal wedding involving a woman vampire and a woman she feeds from during the reception. "Medea" by Carol Leonard is about Hannah and a woman vampire who has come to Hannah in her dreams. They have a tryst during her period and the vampire, Medea, feeds on her menstrual blood; the writing is quite erotic and surprisingly lovely. "Femme-de-Siecle" by Lawrence Schimel is also about a relationship with a vampire where menstrual blood is an issue.

ANTHOLOGIES of VAMPIRE SHORT STORIES

Editors:

Otto Penzler, John Richard Stephens, Ellen Datlow and Terri Windling, Diane Raetz and Patrick Thomas, John Joseph Adams.

THERE ARE MANY good anthologies. Here are five.

The Vampire Archives: The Most Complete Volume of Vampire Tales Ever Published, **edited by Otto Penzler.** This is a fantastic collection of tales. It has a huge section of writings before Dracula, including *Carmilla,* but also twelve other pre-*Dracula* tales. Then there are stories by Anne Rice and Stephen King, and many stories by science fiction writers: Roger Zelazny, Tanith Lee, Brian Stableford, Robert Bloch, Harlan Ellison, H. P. Lovecraft, Ray Bradbury—more than ninety stories and poems in all. It was published in 2009 and is more than a thousand pages in length. But best of all, there is a bibliography at the end, listing vampire novels and short stories up until 2009. Produced by Daniel Seitler, it contains more than five thousand listings. By now it would be more than six thousand.

Vampires, Wine, and Roses: Chilling Tales of Immortal Pleasure, **edited by John Richard Stephens.** This book contains many classic stories and poems as well as essays by famous people. So, it includes Voltaire's listing of vampires in his *Philosophical Dictionary,* poems such as "Lamia" by John Keats, "The Horla" by Guy de Maupassant, and "The Bride of Corinth" by Goethe. It includes offerings from Anne Rice, Stephen King, Woody Allen, Jules Verne, Ray Bradbury, H. G. Wells, and more. A very nice collection.

Teeth: Vampire Tales, **edited by Ellen Datlow and Terri Windling.** This is a book of short stories, marketed as a young adult reader. The stories are really good. There were probably only two I didn't like, and several were truly wonderful. Contributors include Neil Gaiman, Suzy McKee Charnas, Tanith Lee, and Ellen Kushner. The story at the end, by Tanith Lee, "Why Light?" is exquisite and brought tears to my eyes; it involves the quest by vampires to experience the day, and their relationship with vampires who have this ability. "Best Friends Forever" by Cecil Castellucci involves two friends, one human, one vampire, and their decisions about the future, not necessarily what you might think. "Vampire Weather" by Garth Nix is a very unusual story involving fundamentalist Christians and vampires and their entanglements. "Gap Year" by Christopher Barzak is a strange and quite lovely story about energy vampires and the ones that come to a high school. "Late Bloomer" by Suzy McKee Charnas is a very odd story about vampires and creativity—basically they can only imitate and collect. "History" by Ellen Kushner involves a human historian going out with a long-lived vampire who will not tell her what it was really like at various historical events. By the end it is unclear if he wants to forget or really doesn't remember. Will he even remember her? A great collection.

***New Blood,* edited by Diane Raetz and Patrick Thomas.** A mixed bag of vampire short stories, from a cyborg who lives on plasma in "By Any Means" by Danielle Ackley-McPhail, to "Tripp's Raid" by John Sunseri, a story of human and vampire soldiers who work together in strange ways. The best stories are toward the back, I thought, including a wild, funny story written by the editors called "Cannibalistically Incestuous Vampire Penguin from Coney Island." Very experimental and fun. "Tequila Sunset" by Brad Aiken is another rather good story of a turning that didn't turn.

***By Blood We Live,* edited by John Joseph Adams.** A very good anthology of vampire stories by major authors of science fiction, fantasy, and vampire fiction. There are stories by Neil Gaiman, Stephen King, Brian Lumley, Anne Rice, Tanith Lee, Barbara Hambly, and many more. I particularly liked "Life Is the Teacher" by Carrie Vaughn, "The Beautiful, the Damned" by Kristine Kathryn Rusch, "Nunc Dimittis" by Tanith Lee, and "After the Stone Age" by Brian Stableford.

NONFICTION VAMPIRE BOOKS
of INTEREST

Authors:

J. Gordon Melton, Margaret L. Carter, Martin Riccardo, Victoria Nelson, Alan Dundes, Tanya Erzen, Eric Nuzum

I MENTION MANY nonfiction vampire books in Part One. I single out a few here.

The Vampire Book, the Encyclopedia of the Undead, **by J. Gordon Melton.** This is the go-to book for any beginning search. It is vast and has had three editions. The third edition was published in 2011. Whatever you are looking for, folklore, graphic novels, history of Dracula studies, it is all here. Melton became obsessed with vampires at an early age and has a huge collection of books and comic books. But he also has sections on folklore, fanzines, "real" vampires, and almost anything you could imagine. The encyclopedia is more than nine hundred pages and is very useful.

Different Blood: The Vampire as Alien, **by Margaret L. Carter.** This is a book that looks at all the literature (up until 2004, when the book was published) where vampires are a different, alien species. See the Vampires as Other Species, Vampires in Science Fiction, Vampirism as a Disease section for more on this book.

***Liquid Dreams of Vampires,* by Martin V. Riccardo.** This is a fascinating book, published in 1997. Ricardo surveyed people about their dreams and fantasies of vampires, and almost everyone he surveyed didn't just want to meet one, but they also wanted to *be* one. He says both men and women have erotic dreams about vampires. And although women have more of these dreams and fantasies than men, very few of the fantasies mention sexual intercourse; usually the eroticism is about being bitten and sharing blood. He writes that the vampire's lovemaking is often all foreplay, something women want.

***Gothicka: Vampire Heroes, Human Gods, and the New Supernatural,* by Victoria Nelson.** This is a book about the supernatural and Gothic, which she spells with a *k* to distinguish it from medieval cultural aspects. The book explores everything from vampires and zombies to Del Toro's *Hellboy* films and *Pan's Labyrinth*. She says that Gothick pop culture offers one of the only easily accessible bridges to the transcendental, if you are outside of orthodox religion. See Part One for more on Nelson's ideas.

***The Vampire: A Casebook,* by Alan Dundes.** Written in 1998, Dundes collected a serious group of essays by anthropologists, Slavic specialists, folklorists, historians, and more, concentrating on the folklore of the vampire from Greece, Hungary, Romania, and the Balkans. He also includes a wonderful and insightful essay by a forensic psychologist: it says most people really don't experience dead bodies, so many of the stories of bodies that are warm, of blood dripping from the mouth, of groans from the grave, of bodies that even sit up, are actually possible from a medical point of view. It is people's ignorance of death and dying that leads many to assume the dead have become vampires.

***The Dead Travel Fast,* by Eric Nuzum.** This is a light-hearted jaunt through fiction, film, history, and the present. Nuzum traveled to Romania and went to all the supposed Dracula sites. Many have no real historical connection, but he, like Nina Auerbach, understands that vampires address the needs, fears, and concerns of particular times and places.

THE BEST

Authors:

George R. R. Martin, Deborah Harkness, Kimberly Pauley,
Charlie Huston, Chelsea Quinn Yarbro, Jeff Gillenkirk, Nora Roberts,
Terry Prachett, Karen Essex, Dan Simmons, Chloe Neill,
Poppy Z. Brite, Anne Rice, Julie Kagawa.

SO, YOU REALLY don't want to wade through more than 270 vampire novels? Here are a bunch of authors I really enjoyed.

Fevre Dream, **by George R. R. Martin.** A moral vampire hires a Mississippi river boat captain to stop other evil vampires.

A Discovery of Witches, **by Deborah Harkness.** A descendant of Salem witches renounces her magical heritage and becomes an academic researcher in Oxford, England. But when she calls up a book that has been missing for hundreds of years, the supernatural world is alerted and the chase is on.

It Sucks to Be Me **and** *Still Sucks to Be Me,* **by Kimberly Pauley.** A girl finds out her parents are vampires and she must make a difficult choice. Humorous, lovely. In the second book, she makes her choice but her life still sucks.

The Joe Pitt Casebooks series, by Charlie Huston. *Already Dead, No Dominion, Half the Blood of Brooklyn, Every Last Drop,* and *My Dead Body.* A hard-boiled vampire detective struggles to survive in a dystopian, noir New York City. One book takes places mostly on the A train. It feels like New York to this New Yorker.

The Palace, **by Chelsea Quinn Yarbro.** The adventures of the moral vampire Le Comte de Saint-Germain. This one takes place in Florence with political intrigues involving Savonarola and the Medicis.

Pursuit of Darkness, **by Jeff Gillenkirk.** It's a presidential thriller involving a vampire Karl Rove character and a down-and-out reporter.

The Circle Trilogy, by Nora Roberts. This was my favorite series in the romance genre. A team made up of humans, a vampire, a shapeshifter, and a witch, from different lands and time periods, takes on the evil vampire Lilith and her vampire army.

Carpe Jugulum, **by Terry Prachett.** Vampires, witches, and great humor by the British author of the Discworld series. There are some great insights on religion in this book.

***Dracula in Love,* by Karen Essex.** A feminist retelling of the Dracula story; Dracula is not the villain, it's the medical establishment.

***Children of the Night,* by Dan Simmons.** It's a wonderful tale of modern Romania, after the fall of the dictator Nicolae Ceausescu, combining displaced orphans, AIDS, Dracula, and medical science.

The Chicagoland Vampires series, by Chloe Neill. The story of a young woman from a well-connected Chicago political family who is turned against her will and makes the best of it by becoming a sentinel to one of Chicago's three vampire houses. Lots of great Chicago food, politics, and sports.

***Lost Souls,* by Poppy Z. Brite.** It's filled with horror, but the writing is lyrical.

***The Vampire Lestat,* by Anne Rice.** The second book in the Vampire Chronicles and perhaps the best in many ways.

The Blood of Eden series, by Julie Kagawa. It's a dystopian world of vampires and humans with real moral struggles and good writing.

THE LIST:
A COMPLETE LISTING OF THE BOOKS
(Alphabetical by Author)

Books (Fiction)

Adrian, Lara. *Kiss of Midnight* (New York: Dell, 2007).

Ambroziak, K. P. *The Fifth Empire: The Journal of Vincent du Maurier* (K. P. Ambroziak, 2013).

Andrews, Ilona. *Magic Bites* (New York: Ace, 2007).

Arthen, Inanna. The Vampires of New England series: *Mortal Touch* (Pepperell, MA: Light Unseen, 2007) and *The Longer the Fall* (Pepperell, MA: Light Unseen, 2010).

Atwater-Rhodes, Amelia. The Den of Shadows Quartet: *In the Forests of the Night* (New York: Laurel Leaf, 1999), *Demon in My View* (New York: Laurel Leaf, 2000), *Shattered Mirror* (New York: Laurel Leaf, 2001), *Midnight Predator* (New York: Laurel Leaf, 2002).

Banks, L. A. *Minion* (London: Gollancz, 2004), *The Awakening* (New York: St. Martin's, 2004), and *The Hunted* (New York: St. Martin's, 2005).

Bartlett, Gerry. *Real Vampires Have Curves* (New York: Berkeley, 2007).

Brewer, Heather. The Chronicles of Vladimir Tod: *Eighth Grade Bites* (New York: Speak, 2007), *Ninth Grade Slays* (New York: Speak, 2008), *Tenth Grade Bleeds* (New York: Speak, 2009), *Eleventh Grade Burns* (New York: Speak, 2010), *Twelfth Grade Kills* (New York: Speak, 2010).

Briggs, Patricia. The Mercy Thompson series: *Moon Called* (New York: Ace, 2006), *Blood Bound* (New York: Ace, 2007), *Iron Kissed* (New York: Ace, 2008), *Bone Crossed* (New York: Ace, 2009), *Silver Borne* (New York: Ace, 2010), *River Marked* (New York: Ace, 2011).

Brite, Poppy Z. *Lost Souls* (New York: Dell, 1992).

Brotherton, James Patrick. *Reclaiming the Dead* (North Charleston, SC: CreateSpace, 2012).

Brust, Steven. *Agyar* (New York: Tor Books, 1993).

Butcher, Jim. The Dresden Files: *Storm Front* (New York: Roc, 2000) and *Blood Rites* (New York: Roc, 2004).

Butler, Octavia. *Fledgling* (New York: Seven Stories, 2005).

Cabot, Meg. *Insatiable* (New York: William Morrow, 2010).

Caine, Rachel. The Morganville Vampires series: *Glass Houses* (New York: NAL Jam, 2006).

Carter, Margaret L. *Dark Changeling* (Amherst Junction, WI: Hard Shell Word Factory, 1999), *Child of Twilight* (Amherst Junction, WI: Hard Shell Word Factory, 2003).

Cast, P. C., and Kristin Cast. The House of Night series: *Marked* (New York: St. Martin's, 2007), *Betrayed* (New York: St. Martin's, 2007), *Chosen* (New York: St. Martin's, 2008), *Untamed* (New York: St. Martin's, 2008), *Hunted* (New York: St. Martin's,

2009), *Tempted* (New York: St. Martin's, 2009), *Burned* (New York: St. Martin's, 2010).

Channing, Wynne. *What Kills Me* (n.p.: Jet and Jack Press, 2012).

Charnas, Suzy McKee. *The Vampire Tapestry* (New York: Orb, 1980).

Cole, Kresley. The Immortals After Dark series: *Lothaire* (New York: Pocket Books, 2012).

Collins, Nancy A. *Sunglasses After Dark* (Stone Mountain, GA: White Wolf Publishing, 1989, revised 2012), *In the Blood* (Stone Mountain, GA: White Wolf Publishing, 1992).

Cronin, Justin. *The Passage* (New York: Ballantine, 2010).

Davidson, MaryJanice. *Undead and Unwed* (New York: Berkeley Sensation, 2004).

de la Cruz, Melissa. *Bluebloods* (New York: Hyperion, 2007), *Masquerade* (New York: Hyperion, 2008), *Revelations* (New York: Hyperion, 2009), *The Van Allen Legacy* (New York: Hyperion, 2010).

Del Toro, Guillermo, and Chuck Hogan. *The Strain* (New York: Harper, 2009).

Due, Tananarive. *My Soul to Keep* (New York: Harper Collins, 1997).

Eidus, Janice. *The Last Jewish Virgin: A Novel of Fate* (Pasadena, CA: Red Hen Press, 2010).

Elizabeth Kostova, *The Historian* (New York: Little, Brown and Co., 2005).

Elrod, P. N. The Vampire Files series: *Bloodlist* (New York: Ace, 1990), *Lifeblood* (New York: Ace, 1990), *Bloodcircle* (New York: Ace, 1990), *Art in the Blood* (New York: Ace, 1991), *Fire in the Blood* (New York: Ace, 1991), *Blood on the Water* (New York: Ace, 1992).

Essex, Karen. *Dracula in Love* (New York: Doubleday, 2010).

Farnsworth, Christopher. *Blood Oath* (New York: G. P. Putnam's Sons, 2010), *The President's Vampire* (New York: G. P. Putnam's Sons, 2011), *Red, White, and Blood* (New York: G. P. Putnam's Sons, 2012).

Feehan, Christine. *The Dark Prince* (New York: Avon, 1999).

Forsyth, Alan. *The Loneliest Vampire in NYC* (n.p.: Urban Publishing, 2011).

Frost, Jeaniene. The Night Huntress series: *Halfway to the Grave* (New York: Avon, 2007), *One Foot in the Grave* (New York: Avon, 2008), *At Grave's End* (New York: Avon, 2009), *Destined for an Early Grave* (New York: Avon, 2009), *This Side of the Grave* (New York: Avon, 2011).

Fuentes, Carlos. *Vlad,* English ed. (Champaign, IL: Dalkey Archive Press, 2012).

Gaiman, Neil. *The Graveyard Book* (New York: HarperCollins, 2008).

Gillenkirk, Jeff. *Pursuit of Darkness* (San Francisco: Nine Mile Press, 2011).

Grahame-Smith, Seth. *Abraham Lincoln: Vampire Hunter* (New York: Grand Central Publishing, 2010).

Gray, Claudia. *Evernight* (New York: HarperTeen, 2008), *Stargazer* (New York: HarperTeen, 2009), *Hourglass* (New York: HarperTeen, 2010).

Griffith, Susan, and Clay Griffith. The Vampire Empire series: *The Greyfriar* (New York: Pyr, 2010), *The Rift Walker* (2011), *The Kingmakers* (New York: Pyr, 2012).

Haig, Matt. *The Radleys* (New York: Free Press, 2010).

Hambly, Barbara. *Those Who Hunt the Night* (New York: Del Ray, 1998).

Hamilton, Laurell K. The Anita Blake Vampire Hunter series: *Guilty Pleasures* (New York: Jove, 1993), *Laughing Corpse* (New York: Jove,1994), *Circus of the Damned* (New York: Jove,1995), *The Lunatic Café* (New York: Jove,1996), *Bloody Bones* (New York: Jove,1996), *The Killing Dance* (New York: Jove,1997), *Burnt Offerings* (New York: Jove, 1998), *Blue Moon* (New York: Jove,1998), *Obsidian Butterfly* (New York: Jove, 2000), *Narcissus in Chains* (New York: Jove, 2001).

Harkness, Deborah. All Souls Trilogy: *A Discovery of Witches* (New York: Penguin, 2011), *Shadow of Night* (New York: Penguin, 2012).

Harper, Molly. The Jane Jameson series: *Nice Girls Don't Have Fangs* (New York: Pocket Star, 2009), *Nice Girls Don't Date Dead Men* (New York: Pocket Star, 2009), *Nice Girls Don't Live Forever* (New York: Pocket Star, 2009).

Harris, Charlaine. The Southern Vampire Mysteries series: *Dead Until Dark* (New York: Ace, 2001), *Living Dead in Dallas* (New York: Ace, 2002), *Club Dead* (New York: Ace, 2003), *Dead to the World* (New York: Ace, 2004), *Dead as a Doornail* (New York: Ace, 2005), *Definitely Dead* (New York: Ace, 2006), *Altogether Dead* (New York: Ace, 2007), *From Dead to Worse* (New York: Ace, 2008), *Dead and Gone* (New York: Ace, 2009), *Dead in the Family* (New York: Ace, 2010), *Dead Reckoning* (New York: Ace, 2011), *Deadlocked* (New York: Ace, 2012), *Dead Ever After* (New York: Ace, 2013).

Harrison, Kim. The Hollows series: *Dead Witch Walking* (New York: Harper Voyager, 2004).

Hocking, Amanda. The My Blood Approves series: *My Blood Approves* (North Charleston, SC: CreateSpace, 2010), *Fate* (North Charleston, SC: CreateSpace, 2010), *Flutter* (North Charleston, SC: CreateSpace, 2010), *Wisdom* (North Charleston, SC: CreateSpace, 2010), *Letters to Elise: A Peter Townsend Novella* (North Charleston, SC: CreateSpace, 2010).

Hubbard, Susan. *The Society of S* (New York: Simon & Schuster, 2007), *The Year of Disappearances* (New York: Simon & Schuster, 2008), *The Season of Risks* (New York: Simon & Schuster, 2010).

Huff, Tanya. The Blood Books series: *Brood Price* (New York: DAW, 1991), *Blood Trail* (New York: DAW, 1992), *Blood Lines* (New York: DAW, 1993), *Blood Pact* (New York: DAW, 1993), *Blood Debt* (New York: DAW, 1997), *Smoke and Shadows* (New York: DAW, 2004), *Smoke and Mirrors* (New York: DAW, 2005), *Smoke and Ashes* (New York: DAW, 2006).

Hunter, Faith. The Jane Yellowrock series: *Skinwalker* (New York: Roc, 2009), *Blood Cross* (New York: Roc, 2010).

Huston, Charlie. The Joe Pitt Casebook series: *Already Dead* (New York: Ballantine Books, 2005), *No Dominion* (New York: Del Rey, 2006), *Half the Blood of Brooklyn* (New York: Del Rey, 2007), *Every Last Drop* (New York: Del Rey, 2008), *My Dead Body* (New York: Del Rey, 2009).

Jinks, Catherine. *The Reformed Vampire Support Group* (Orlando, FL: Houghton Mifflin Harcourt, 2009).

Johnson, Alaya. *Moonshine* (New York: St. Martin's, 2010), *Wicked City* (New York: Thomas Dunne, 2012).

Josephson, Wayne. *Emma and the Vampires* (Naperville, IL: Sourcebooks Landmark, 2010).

Juers, S. L. *Eternally Yours* (Bloomington, IN: AuthorHouse, 2005).

Kagawa, Julie. The Blood of Eden series: *The Immortal Rules* (Don Mills, Ontario: Harlequin Teen, 2012), *The Eternity Cure* (Don Mills, Ontario: Harlequin Teen, 2013).

King, Stephen. *'Salem's Lot* (New York: Doubleday, 1975).

Klause, Annette Curtis. *The Silver Kiss* (New York: Delacorte, 1990).

Lindqvist, John Ajvide. *Let the Right One In*, English ed. (New York: Thomas Dunne, 2007).

Lukyanenko, Sergei. *Night Watch* (New York: Hyperion, 2006) and *Day Watch* (New York: Hyperion, 2007).

Matheson, Robert. *I Am Legend*, reprint ed. (orig. pub 1954; New York: Tor, 1995).

McDermott, Morna. *The Sacrament* (n.p.: Morna McDermott, 2011).

McKinley, Robin. *Sunshine* (New York: Speak, 2003).

Mead, Richelle. The Vampire Academy series: *Vampire Academy* (New York: Razorbill, 2007), *Frostbite* (New York: Razorbill, 2008), *Shadow Kiss* (New York: Razorbill, 2008), *Blood Promise* (New York: Razorbill, 2009).

Meehl, Brian. *Suck It Up* (New York: Delacorte, 2008).

Meyer, Stephenie. The Twilight Saga: *Twilight* (New York: Little, Brown and Co., 2005), *New Moon* (New York: Little, Brown and Co., 2006), *Eclipse* (New York: Little, Brown and Co., 2007), *Breaking Dawn* (New York: Little, Brown and Co.,

2008), *Midnight Sun* (never released; 2008), *The Short Second Life of Bree Tanner* (New York: Little, Brown and Co., 2010).

Moore, Christopher. *Bloodsucking Fiends: A Love Story* (New York: Simon & Schuster, 1995), *You Suck: A Love Story* (New York: Simon & Schuster, 2007), *Bite Me: A Love Story* (New York: Simon & Schuster, 2010).

Mosiman, Billie Sue. *Red Moon Rising* (New York: DAW, 2001), *Malachi's Moon* (New York: DAW, 2002), *Craven Moon* (New York: DAW, 2003).

Munson, Trevor O. *Angel of Vengeance* (London: Titan, 2011).

Neill, Chloe. The Chicagoland Vampires series: *Some Girls Bite* (New York: NAL Trade, 2009), *Friday Night Bites* (New York: NAL Trade, 2009), *Twice Bitten* (New York: NAL Trade, 2010), *Hard Bitten* (New York: NAL Trade, 2011), *Drink Deep* (New York: NAL Trade, 2011), *Biting Cold* (New York: NAL Trade, 2012), *House Rules* (New York: NAL Trade, 2013), *Biting Bad* (New York: NAL Trade, 2013).

Newman, Kim. The Anno Dracula series: *Anno Dracula* (London: Titan, 1992), *The Bloody Red Baron* (London: Titan, 1995), *Anno Dracula 1959, or The Judgment of Tears* (London: Titan, 1998), *Anno Dracula: Johnny Alucard* (London: Titan, 2013).

Nicolai, Mel, and Jana Perinchief. *The Shake* (North Charleston, SC: CreateSpace, 2010).

Noël, Alyson. The Immortals series: *Evermore* (New York: St. Martin's, 2009).

Oates, Joyce Carol. *The Accursed* (New York: HarperCollins, 2013).

Pauley, Kimberly. *Sucks to Be Me* (Renton, WA: Mirrorstone, 2008), *Still Sucks to Be Me* (Renton, WA: Mirrorstone, 2010).

Pike, Christopher. *Thirst* (New York: Simon Pulse, 2009).

Powers, Tim. *The Stress of Her Regard* (San Francisco: Tachyon, 1989).

Pratchett, Terry. *Carpe Jugulum* (New York: HarperTorch, 1998), *Monstrous Regiment* (New York: HarperTorch, 2003).

Quinn Yarbro, Chelsea. *Hôtel Transylvania* (New York: St. Martin's, 1978), *The Palace* (New York: Warner, 1978), *Blood Games* (New York: Warner, 1979).

Rardin, Jennifer. The Jaz Parks series: *Once Bitten, Twice Shy* (New York: Orbit, 2007).

Rex, Adam. *Fat Vampire: A Never Coming of Age Story* (New York: Balzer + Bray, 2010).

Rice, Anne. The Vampire Chronicles: *Interview with the Vampire* (New York: Ballantine, 1976), *The Vampire Lestat* (New York: Ballantine, 1985), *Queen of the Damned* (New York: Ballantine, 1988), *Tale of the Body Thief* (New York: Ballantine, 1992), *Memnoch the Devil* (New York: Ballantine, 1995), *The Vampire Armand* (New York: Ballantine, 1998), *Merrick* (New York: Ballantine, 2000), *Black and Gold* (New York: Ballantine, 2001).

Roberts, Nora. The Circle Trilogy: *Morrigan's Cross* (New York: Jove, 2006), *Dance of the Gods* (New York: Jove, 2006), *Valley of Silence* (New York: Jove, 2006).

Rock, Rebecca. *Daywalker* (Lincoln, NE: iUniverse, 2007).

Rymer, James Malcolm. *Varney the Vampire, Or the Feast of Blood* (orig. pub 1845–47; n.p.: Zittaw, 2007).

Saberhagen, Fred. *The Dracula Tape* (New York: Tor, 1975), *An Old Friend of the Family* (New York: Tor Fantasy, 1979), *The Holmes-Dracula File* (New York: Tor Fantasy, 1978).

Sands, Lynsay. The Argeneau Vampire series: *Single White Vampire* (New York: Avon, 2003), *Love Bites* (New York: Avon, 2004), *Tall, Dark & Hungry* (New York: Avon, 2004), *A Quick Bite* (New York: Avon, 2005), *A Bite to Remember* (New York: Avon, 2006), *Bite Me If You Can* (New York: Avon, 2007), *The Accidental Vampire* (New York: Avon, 2008), *Vampires Are Forever* (New York: Avon, 2008), *Vampire, Interrupted* (New York: Avon, 2008).

Scott, Kathryn Leigh. *Dark Passages* (Beverly Hills: Pomegranate Press, 2011).

Scully, B. E. *Verland: The Transformation* (n.p.: BE Scully, 2011).

Shan, Darren. The Darren Shan Saga: Cirque du Freak series: *Cirque du Freak: A Living Nightmare* (New York: Little, Brown and Co., 2000), *The Vampire's Assistant* (New York: Little, Brown and Co., 2001), *Tunnels of Blood* (New York: Little, Brown and Co., 2002).

Shepard, Lucius. *The Golden* (New York: Bantam,1993).

Sheridan Le Fanu, Joseph. *Carmilla* (1872).

Sherman, Beck. *Revamp* (n.p.: Beck Sherman, 2009).

Simmons, Dan. *Children of the Night* (New York: St. Martin's, 1992), *Carrion Comfort* (orig. pub. 1989; important new intro in reprint ed., New York: St. Martin's, 2009).

Smith, L. J. The Night World series: *Secret Vampire, Daughters of Darkness, Spellbinder* (New York: Simon Pulse, 1996); The Vampire Diaries series: *The Awakening* (New York: Harper Teen, 1991), *The Struggle* (New York: HarperCollins, 1991), *The Fury* (New York: HarperCollins, 1991), *Dark Reunion* (New York: HarperCollins, 1992).

Sosnowski, David. *Vamped* (New York: Free Press, 2004).

Stratford, Sarah Jane. *The Midnight Guardian* (New York: St. Martin's, 2009).

Strieber, Whitley. A Vampire's Life series: *The Hunger* (New York: Pocket Books, 1981), *The Last Vampire* (New York: Pocket Books, 2001), *Lilith's Dream* (New York: Pocket Books, 2003).

Sturgeon, Theodore. *Some of Your Blood* (orig. pub. 1961; New York: Caroll & Graf, 1994).

Talbot, Michael. *The Delicate Dependency: A Novel of the Vampire Life* (New York: Avon,1982).

Taylor, Terence. *Bite Marks* (New York: St. Martin's, 2009), *Blood Pressure* (New York: St. Martin's, 2010).

Teague, Gypsey. *Fangs & Claws* (North Charleston, SC: CreateSpace, 2012).

Van Patten, Steven. *Brookwater's Curse* vol. I (Bloomington, IN: AuthorHouse, 2005).

Vande Velde, Vivian. *Companions of the Night* (orig. pub. 1995; Orlando: Magic Carpet Books, 2002).

Vargas, Fred. *An Uncertain Place*, English ed. (New York, Penguin: 2011).

Vaughn, Carrie. The Kitty Norville series: *Kitty and the Midnight Hour* (New York: Grand Central Publishing, 2005), *Kitty Goes to Washington* (York: Grand Central Publishing, 2006), *Kitty Takes a Holiday* (York: Grand Central Publishing, 2007), *Kitty and the Silver Bullet* (York: Grand Central Publishing, 2008), *Kitty and the Dead Man's Hand* (York: Grand Central Publishing, 2009), *Kitty Raises Hell* (York: Grand Central Publishing, 2009), *Kitty's House of Horrors*

(York: Grand Central Publishing, 2010), *Kitty Goes to War* (York: Grand Central Publishing, 2010), *Kitty's Big Trouble* (York: Grand Central Publishing, 2011).

Ward, J. R. The Black Dagger Brotherhood series: *Dark Lover* (New York: Signet, 2005).

Westerfeld, Scott. *Peeps* (New York: Razorbill, 2005).

Wilson, Colin. *Space Vampires* (orig. pub. 1976; Rhinebeck, NY: Monkfish, 2009).

Workman, RaShelle. The Blood and Snow series vols. 1–4: *Blood and Snow, Revenant in Training, The Vampire Christopher, Blood Soaked Promises* (Bountiful, UT: Polished Pen Press, 2012).

Yeovil, Jack (a.k.a. Kim Newman). The Vampire Geneviève series: *Dachenfels* (Nottingham, UK: Games Workshop, 1989), *Geneviève Undead* (Nottingham, UK: Games Workshop, 1993), *Beasts in Velvet* (Nottingham, UK: Games Workshop, 1993), *Silver Nails* (Nottingham, UK: Games Workshop, 2002).

Anthologies

Adams, John Joseph, editor. *By Blood We Live* (San Francisco, Night Shade Books, 2009).

Datlow, Ellen, and Terri Windling, editors. *Teeth: Vampire Tales* (New York: HarperCollins, 2011).

Harris, Charlaine, and Toni. L. P. Kelner, editors. *Many Blood Returns* (New York: Ace, 2007).

Keesey, Pam, editor. *Daughters of Darkness, Lesbian Vampire Stories* (San Francisco: Cleis Press, 1993), *Dark Angels: Lesbian Vampire Erotica* (San Francisco: Cleis Press, 1995).

Penzler, Otto, editor. *The Vampire Archives: The Most Complete Volume of Vampire Tales Ever Published* (New York: Vintage, 2009).

Raetz, Diane, and Patrick Thomas, editors. *New Blood* (n.p.: Padwolf Publishing, 2010).

Stephens, John Richard, editor. *Vampires, Wine, and Roses: Chilling Tales of Immortal Pleasure* (New York: Metro, 2008).

Short Stories and Poems

Alecsandri, Vasile. "The Vampire" (1886).

Baudelaire, Charles Pierre. "Les Fleurs du Mal" (1857).

Bierce, Ambrose. "The Death of Halpin Frayser" (1893).

Bradbury, Ray. "October Country" (1955).

Braddon, Mary Elizabeth. "Good Lady Ducayne" (1896).

Byron, Lord George Gordon. "The Giaour" (1813).

Cholmondeley, Mary. "Let Loose" (1890).

Crawford, Anne. "A Mystery of the Campagna" (1887).

de Maupassant, Guy. "The Horla" (1887).

Doyle, Sir Arthur Conan. "John Barrington Cowles" (1884).

Dumas, Alexandre. "The Vampire of the Carpathian Mountains" (1849).

Gilbert, William. "The Last Lords of Gardonal" (1867).

Harris, Charlaine. "A Touch of Dead" (2009).

Hawthorne, Julian. "Ken's Mystery" (1884).

Henderson, Zenna. "Food to All Flesh" (1953).

Keats, John. "Lamia" (1819).

Linton, Elizabeth Lynn. "The Fate of Madame" (1880).

Malory, Sir Thomas. "Le Morte d'Arthur" (1470).

Nisbet, Hume. "The Old Portrait" and "The Vampire Maid" (1890).

Poe, Edgar Allan. "Ligeia" (1838).

Polidori, John William. "The Vampyre" (1819).

Scott, Sir Walter. "Rokeby" (1813).

Southey, Robert. "Thalaba, the Destroyer" (1801).

Stevenson, Robert Louis. "Olalla" (1885).

Turgenev, Ivan. "Phantoms" (1864).

Von Goethe, Johann Wolfgang. "The Bride of Corinth" (1797).

Books (Nonfiction)

Auerbach, Nina. *Our Vampires, Ourselves* (Chicago: University of Chicago Press, 1995).

Badderly, Gavin. *Goth Chic,* (London: Plexus Publishing, 2002).

Carter, Margaret L. *Different Blood: The Vampire as Alien* (n.p.: Amber Quill Press, 2004).

Clements, Susannah. *The Vampire Defanged* (Grand Rapids, MI: Brazos Press, 2011).

Click, Melissa A., Jennifer Stevens Aubrey, and Elizabeth Behm-Morawitz, editors. *Bitten by Twilight: Youth Culture, Media & the Vampire Franchise* (New York: Peter Lang, 2010).

Dundes, Alan. *The Vampire: A Casebook* (Madison, WI: University of Wisconsin Press, 1998).

Dunn, George A., and Rebecca Housel, editors. *Trueblood and Philosophy* (Hoboken, NJ: John Wiley & Sons, 2010).

Durand, Kevin A., editor. *Buffy Meets the Academy: Essays on the Episodes and Scripts as Texts* (Jefferson, NC: McFarland & Co., 2009).

Erzen, Tanya. *Fanpire: The Twilight Saga and the Women Who Love It* (Boston: Beacon Press, 2012).

Housel, Rebecca, and J. Jerem Wisnewsky, editors. *Twilight and Philosophy* (Hoboken, NJ: John Wiley & Sons, 2009).

Jowett, Lorna. *Sex and the Slayer: A Gender Studies Primer for the Buffy Fan* (Middletown, CT: Wesleyan University Press, 2005).

Kaplan, Stephen. *Vampires Are* (Palm Springs: ETC Publications, 1984).

McNally, Raymond T., and Radu Florescu. *In Search of Dracula: The Enthralling History of Dracula and Vampires* (London: Robson Books, 1995).

Melton, Gordon. *The Vampire Book: The Encyclopedia of the Undead,* 3rd ed. (Canton, MI: Visible Ink Press, 2011).

Nelson, Victoria. *Gothicka: Vampire Heroes, Human Gods, and the New Supernatural* (Cambridge: Harvard University Press, 2012).

Nuzum, Eric. *The Dead Travel Fast: Stalking Vampires from Nosferatu to Count Chocula* (New York: St. Martin's, 2007).

Poole, Robert. *Earthrise: How Man First Saw the Earth* (New Haven: Yale University Press, 2008).

Ramsland, Katherine. *The Vampire Companion: The Official Guide to Anne Rice's the Vampire Chronicles* (New York: Ballantine, 1993), *Piercing the Darkness: Undercover with Vampires in America Today* (New York: HarperPrism, 1998).

Riccardo, Martin V. *Liquid Dreams of Vampires* (St. Paul, MN: Llewellyn, 1997).

Taylor, Bron. *Dark Green Religion: Nature Spirituality and the Planetary Future.* (Berkeley: University of California Press, 2010).

Wilson, Colin. *The Outsider* (London: Gollancz, 1967).

AFTERWORD

NOW THAT FOUR YEARS have passed, and I have returned to "sanity" and actually read a bunch of other books besides vampire novels (although I still plan to read the next volumes in my favorite series—All Souls, Chicagoland, Blood of Eden—and any vampire novel highly, highly recommended), I look back and consider, what did those four years bring me?

The truth is that when you follow something simple to its core, you find it connected to so many things. It's just like that wonderful quote from the California naturalist and writer John Muir: "When we try and pick out anything by itself, we find it hitched to everything else in the universe."

I started with vampires, but it brought me the world. Whatever you obsess on, I hope that happens for you, too.

ACKNOWLEDGMENTS

THIS BOOK WOULD never have been published, nor would I have given workshops and sermons and talks on this topic, if I hadn't sat by the bedside of my late, wonderful husband, John Lowell Gliedman, my partner for thirty-five years, and meditated on mortality and immortality as he lay dying. We also watched *Moonlight* together, the wonderful television show about a moral vampire detective, that had only one season on CBS.

I am indebted to the Pagan community and its festivals, and to various Unitarian Universalist churches. They allowed me to try out these ideas in workshops and sermons. Erica Jong led me to Dave Blum at Amazon, who first published some of these ideas as an essay. My neighbor, Larry Kirschbaum, was also instrumental. The Wertheim Study at the New York Public Library gave me a sanctuary to write that was miraculously across the street from my NPR office.

I thank Jane Rotrosen and Meg Ruley, my agents, who gave me great advice and looked over my contract even though I didn't use them for this venture. Also, my dear friends Carol Schrager and June Erlick, who gave sound advice.

Lastly, I am so grateful to Caroline Pincus and all the folks at Red Wheel/Weiser. Unlike several editors and publishers who saw my original proposal and had their own visions for the book, Caroline said they would publish it the way I wanted it—and that was deeply important to me.

ABOUT THE AUTHOR

MARGOT ADLER has been involved with Earth-based spirituality, Wicca, and Paganism since 1972. She is the author of *Drawing Down the Moon*, the classic study of Paganism and Goddess Spirituality, as well as *Heretic's Heart: A Journey Through Spirit and Revolution*. In her mundane life, she is a 35-year veteran correspondent for NPR whose pieces regularly air on *All Things Considered, Morning Edition,* and *Weekend Edition.* She lives in New York City. Visit her at *www.margotadler.com*.

TO OUR READERS